Powerful Celtic Women in History
Warrior Queens, Priestesses, and Wise Women

Elise Baker

Intrepidas Publishing

© Copyright 2024 - All rights reserved.

The content contained within this book may not be reproduced, duplicated or transmitted without direct written permission from the author or the publisher.

Under no circumstances will any blame or legal responsibility be held against the publisher, or author, for any damages, reparation, or monetary loss due to the information contained within this book, either directly or indirectly.

Legal Notice:

This book is copyright protected. It is only for personal use. You cannot amend, distribute, sell, use, quote or paraphrase any part, or the content within this book, without the consent of the author or publisher.

Disclaimer Notice:

Please note the information contained within this document is for educational and entertainment purposes only. All effort has been executed to present accurate, up to date, reliable, complete information. No warranties of any kind are declared or implied. Readers acknowledge that the author is not engaged in the rendering of legal, financial, medical or professional advice. The content within this book has been derived from various sources. Please consult a licensed professional before attempting any techniques outlined in this book.

By reading this document, the reader agrees that under no circumstances is the author responsible for any losses, direct or indirect, that are incurred as a result of the use of the information contained within this document, including, but not limited to, errors, omissions, or inaccuracies.

Contents

1. Introduction — 1
   Why Does History Ignore Women?
   What Did It Mean to Be a Woman in the Celtic World?
   What to Expect From This Book

2. Warrior Queens — 14
   Bravery Beyond Bounds
      Boudica: Leader of a Rebellion Against Rome
      Medb: Queen of Connacht

3. Women Warriors and Peacemakers — 33
      Cartimandua: Diplomat Queen
      Scáthach: The Shadowy One
      Aífe: Warrior Princess
      Liath Luachra: Druidess Warrior

4. Priestesses — 49
   Spiritual Leadership
      Female Spiritual Leadership in Celtic Society
      Brigid the Bright—From Pagan to Christian Saint
      Notable Seeresses and Prophetesses

5. Wise Women　　　　　　　　　　　　　　　　　　67
    Healers, Seers, Poets
        The Celtic Wise Woman
        Beliefs in the Death and Afterlife
        Examples From Celtic Myth
        Learning From Wise Women

6. Powerful Female Figures in Celtic Mythology　　84
    Women, Goddesses, Myth, and Celtic Society
    Rhiannon: Goddess of Sovereignty
    The Morrígan: Goddess of War and Fate
    Ceridwen: Goddess of Poetry, Magic, and Transformation
    Deirdre of the Sorrows: Love Over Duty

7. Conclusion　　　　　　　　　　　　　　　　　　101
    What These Women Can Teach Us
    How Their Stories Inspire Us

About the Author　　　　　　　　　　　　　　　　107
Elise Baker

Also By　　　　　　　　　　　　　　　　　　　　109

References and Bibliography　　　　　　　　　　　112

Chapter One
Introduction

A whole band of foreigners will be unable to cope with one [Gaul] in a fight, if he calls in his wife, stronger than he by far and with flashing eyes; least of all when she swells her neck and gnashes her teeth, and poising her huge white arms, begins to rain blows mingled with kicks, like shots discharged by the twisted cords of a catapult.
– Ammianus Marcellinus

THE CELTS, A COHESIVE group of tribes inked by common cultural practices, lived in Europe during the Iron Age between 700 B.C.E. and 400 C.E. Like in all great civilizations, women had a key role to play in their society.

In this book, we will introduce the remarkable female figures of ancient Celtic history, real and mythological, whose legacies have influenced the contemporary women's rights movement. Our discussion will highlight their stories and accomplishments as well as how they influenced each other. By placing these leaders in their historical context, we will also highlight the challenges and opportunities they faced compared to those of today.

Below, we explore why history has ignored women and how this book will begin to redress the imbalance.

Why Does History Ignore Women?

Why are there so few accounts of women and the role they have played throughout time? Why do they still tend to be absent from history books today?

One answer is the "great man" theory that 19th-century historians popularized. They proposed that most of history can be explained by the impact of great men or heroes. These individuals had superior natural attributes, such as a strong intellect, heroic courage, or divine inspiration, which had a decisive effect on their leadership abilities and resulted in them having a decisive effect on world events. Thus, accounts of the past were generally written by men and focused on achievements in the public sphere—the areas of war, politics, diplomacy, and administration.

In his book *On Heroes, Hero-Worship, and the Heroic in History*, essayist, historian, and philosopher (Thomas Carlyle 1841: 1–2) explained that:

> Universal History, the history of what man has accomplished in this world, is... the History of Great Men... They were the leaders of men, these great ones; the modelers, patterns, and in a wide sense creators, of whatsoever the general mass of men contrived to do or to attain... the embodiment, of Thoughts that dwelt in the Great Men sent into the world: the soul of the whole world's history, it may justly be considered, we the history of these.

Women were usually excluded from the annals of so-called "great men," and, if they were mentioned at all, they were generally portrayed in stereotypical gender roles such as wives, mothers, daughters, and mistresses.

When the academic discipline of women's history emerged in the late 1960s and early 1970s, it became clear that women had been neglected in the wider field because historians had viewed it to be almost singularly about exercising and transmitting power. This meant that the subject of study was often politics and economics, arenas in which almost all the actors were men (Rose, 2010).

In recent times, researchers have done a lot to discover more about how women lived in the past. The rise of women's history coincided with an increased interest in social history, which is based on the idea that an understanding of the everyday lives of ordinary people is just as important to making sense of the past as the analysis of significant political and military events (Rose, 2010). Greater knowledge of social history has therefore helped women's history emerge from the shadows.

In addition, a new focus and appreciation of the diverse roles women have occupied in the past has led to the rediscovery of the positions they have occupied as leaders throughout history. This book contributes to this exploration and helps to redress the imbalance by profiling several women in leadership roles, such as Boudica, the British warrior queen, and Cartimandua, the first-century queen of the Brigantes. It also looks at the many other roles women played in ancient Celtic society, ranging from poetesses to priestesses to healers.

What Did It Mean to Be a Woman in the Celtic World?

Today, North American and European societies are relatively egalitarian, with the sexes enjoying equal rights. However, for much of history, this was not the case, as men were considered superior to women. In many societies, the former had limited rights and were not allowed freedoms such as the right to vote or own property.

Significantly, in the Celtic world women appear to have been treated as equals to men. It may have even been better to be a woman then than it is to be one today, considering the Celts believed in sexual freedom for all, making them one of the most permissive societies in history.

Historians agree that Celtic women were valued and had a prominent position in society, where they often assumed leadership positions in their tribes, such as wise women. This was influenced by their mythological system, which cast women in the role of mediators between the mortal realm and the Otherworld. However, experts do not all agree on the extent of Celtic women's equality with men.

Some believe that women had something approaching freedom but remained the inferior sex. These researchers argue that, while they had some liberties in Celtic society, it may not be the case that they had entirely the same status as men. Notably, Caesar observes that husbands had the "power of life and death" over their wives and children. It may have also been the case that Celtic women's standing changed after the Roman Conquest due to the influence of the Empire's law and culture, which positioned the man as the head of the household.

On balance though, the testimony of Classical authors, archaeological findings, and myth all suggest that some high-ranking Celtic women enjoyed a position comparable to that of their male peers (Green, 1997). Meanwhile, most believe that women enjoyed a prominent position in society and full equality with the opposite sex, especially in the centuries before the Roman Conquest.

This position is supported by the existence of female leaders such as Boudica and anthropological arguments. For example, the Celts were a matrilineal society. In such systems, men marry women who are around their age, whereas, in patrilineal systems, there is a much greater age gap between partners. Additionally, although men did the hunting, it was women who sowed and harvested the crops, so they had high prestige compared to those societies where men alone provided the food (Watts, 2005; Sullivan, 2024).

Goddesses also occupied important roles in the Celtic religious system, and this may have been reflective of their importance. However, it must be acknowledged that societies where women were inferior to men, like ancient Greece, also had both male and female deities.

Irish myth, reflecting the fact that women in Celtic Ireland enjoyed the same freedoms as men, presents instances that illustrate equality between women and men in Celtic society. For example, the great Irish epic "The Táin" ("The Cattle Raid of Cooley") refers to the dominant role of women throughout its narrative. The tale proves that both sexes played decisive roles in Irish culture and, in some cases, that women even held more power and influence (Flisiuk, 2015).

In the text, women use their power, physicality, sexuality, wealth, and occasionally, supernatural abilities to prove that they are equal to men. Men are presented as the strongest and most important characters; however, their powers are weakened when they come under the influence of women. The male heroes of the epic, Cú Chulainn, Conchobar mac Nessa, and Ailill mac Máta would also not have achieved anything if it were not for the efforts of their female counterparts, Medb, Macha, and Fedelm.

Another example that can be found in "The Táin" is that women were able to initiate divorce if they wanted to and were not punished if they were unfaithful to their husbands. One of the main characters in the saga, Queen Medb, demonstrates this, as she had been married two or three times before she wed her husband in the text, King Ailill of Connacht.

During her previous marriages, she'd had extramarital affairs and also took several lovers between spouses. This conduct would have been severely condemned if she had lived in ancient Greece or ancient Rome; however, in Irish society, Queen Medb held a strong position of power and influence that rivaled that of her Ailill. Notably, their relationship is portrayed as a power struggle rather than one of a man served by a loving wife, as the quote that Medb's "words were sharp; they cut him deep, in a war between the sheets" suggests (Flisiuk, 2015).

The egalitarian and permissive nature of Celtic society is clear in how women were allowed more than one sexual partner and had more freedom over their sexuality than was the case in other ancient civilizations. Julius Caesar reported on this, explaining that:

> Groups of ten or twelve men have wives together in common, particularly brothers along with brothers, and fathers with sons; but the children born of these unions are considered to belong to the family of the man [the wife] was married to. (Watts, 2005: 14)

Dio confirms that women enjoyed expressing their sensuality in Celtic society, recalling a conversation he'd had in the third century C.E. with Julia Domna, mother of the emperor Caracalla and wife of the Caledonian chieftain Argentocoxus, who told Dio that "we consort openly with the best men" (Watts, 2005: 14).

The freedom women enjoyed meant that their menfolk could not always be certain who the father of a child was. For this reason, succession within Celtic tribes and clans was matrilineal, so inheritance traveled through the female line. Furthermore, as men were often lost in combat and frequently did not live to see their offspring grow up, it made more sense for children to inherit through their mothers (French, 2020).

Examples of Powerful Women in the Celtic World

Extremely powerful and influential women could and did exist in Celtic Europe. There were not many, but they were accepted. Female leaders are common in Celtic myths and legends, and they are evidenced in historical sources.

Classical writers tell us that prominent women were commonplace in Iron Age Britain. In his *Agricola XVI*, Tacitus made a point of mentioning that the Britons did not care what gender their leaders were and that they had told him specifically that female commanders were commonplace (Green, 1997).

Celtic women could choose to be trained as warriors if they wanted to, and some even went on to become trainers themselves. One Irish myth tells of sisters, (or twin sisters) Scáthach and Aífe, who owned rival warrior training camps. Scáthach is also a legendary Scottish warrior who appears in the *Ulster Cycle* and trains the hero Cú Chulainn. Andraste, another example from myth, is the Celtic war goddess that Boudica invokes while fighting against the Romans in 61 C.E.

Additionally, according to historical sources, women were a common site on the battlefields, as demonstrated by a witness account written by a Roman soldier. The man reported that female warriors were "equal to any Roman man in hand-to-hand combat" and were beautiful as well as strong. The same observer appears to have rated Celtic women above their Roman counterparts, reporting that the latter "pale in comparison" (Walsh, 2015).

Diodorus Siculus observed that Gaulish women were just as brave as their menfolk: "The women of the Gauls are not only like men in their great stature, but they are a match for them in courage as well" (Walsh, 2015). All Roman accounts seem to agree that Celtic women were large, definitely taller than Roman women and, some say, larger than most men. Possessing these qualities meant that women could become formidable warriors and were often more feared by invading Roman armies than their menfolk were.

However, it is important to note that the Romans believed that the presence of women in positions of authority was an indication of a weak society. It was said that: "If a man is subject to a queen—a *dux femina*—he is disgraced, and the only way to erase this shame is to conquer her" (Mc-Coppin, 2022: 27).

Archaeological Evidence

Archaeological evidence also supports the idea that there were women leaders in the Celtic world.

It is possible to tell whether discovered remains or graves belonged to someone of high status due to the goods they were buried with, the jewelry they wore, or articles of clothing that have survived and been preserved. Torcs were an indicator of social rank within the Celtic tribes, as were tattoos, which were sometimes associated with aristocratic status. At other times, these bodily modifications were reflective of low status. Both Julius Caesar and Strabo describe how the Celts created them using a blue dye made from woad (Simmons, 2012).

Graves from Iron Age Europe point to the presence of independent, high-ranking women, who may well have been dynastic rulers in their own right. One example is the grave of the Lady of Vix. This was a woman who lived at the end of the sixth century B.C.E. and was 35 years old when she died. She had lived in Vix, northern Burgundy, France, and was buried at the foot of a hill where the early Iron Age settlement of Mount Lassois was located.

Her burial is notable because archaeological evidence suggests that she had been buried with great ceremony and reverence. Her body had been carried to the tomb on a great four-wheeled bier that was then dismantled and placed with her in her tomb (Green, 1997). She had also been interred with many luxurious grave goods, including jewelry and other artifacts.

One such item was an enormous bronze krater (wine-making vessel) which stood at 5 feet, and it would have been manufactured in Corinth in Greece or Eturia in Italy. Despite its size, it would have been transported across the Alps to northern Burgundy. Due to the craftsmanship involved in making it and how it was transported across Europe, the presence of the krater in the woman's tomb is indicative of her high rank. The vessel implies that she had strong links with the Mediterranean world, either because she was from there herself or because it was a gift to her from another ruler (Green, 1997). The evidence therefore suggests that the Lady of Vix is an example of an autonomous female ruler in the Celtic world.

The Lady of Vix is not the only example of an early Iron Age woman buried with elaborate rituals and luxurious grave goods. In the fourth century B.C.E., a lady was buried at Reinheim beside the Blies River in Germany. She had been laid to rest with a set of gold ring-shaped jewelry, including a torc and armlets, all of which were intricately decorated with metalwork engravings. The accessories suggest that she was either important enough to commission jewelry or the members of her community believed her to have a high or divine status (Green, 1997; Sullivan, 2024).

The metal adornments were decorated with images of a woman with her hands folded on her stomach in the manner of a corpse. There were also great birds of prey perched on top of her head, which is indicative of the depicted figure's divine status. While this iconography may represent a goddess, it could also depict the buried woman herself.

The equality women enjoyed during the Celtic period came to an end after the Romans extended their empire across Europe in the first centuries B.C.E and C.E. and converted Celtic society into a patriarchal one, imposing the view that men were superior to women and ending egalitarianism in the Celtic regions until recent times.

Everyday Lives of Celtic Women

The Celts were divided into tribal groups and lived in small settlements across Europe that were united by common cultural and spiritual beliefs. They were an agrarian society whose livelihood was dependent on the land, and their consequent close affinity with nature has led some historians to speculate that their gods and goddesses were forces of nature rather than people.

It is difficult to know what the everyday lives of Celtic women were like. Not much information survives about them, as their society had a verbal rather than a written tradition. Consequently, most of the information we have about this ancient group comes from Classical writings by Greek and Roman commentators, many of whom were hostile toward the Celts and lacked understanding of their culture. As mentioned above, some archaeological evidence survives that reflects that women were often buried with combs and jewelry, which were indicative of their status and vanity.

However, the limited amount we do know about the daily lives of Celtic women suggests that they enjoyed an equal status with men. Public life was primarily the domain of men, but women were able to practice any occupation. This meant that they could be Druids, including priestesses, poets, and healers, and they could conduct business without the involvement of their fathers or husbands. They could also be warriors or political ambassadors.

One account of a woman acting as an ambassador arose when a woman (whose name does not survive) negotiated the treaty between the Carthaginian general Hannibal and the Celtic Volcae during a march against Rome. According to Plutarch, writing in the second century C.E., there was a long-standing tradition of Celtic women acting as judges or mediators in political and military disputes. Reports also state that they played a mediating role in tribal assemblies.

Women were valued in Celtic society, as demonstrated by the rights they were given in marriage. The Celts saw marriage as a partnership between a man and a woman, unlike the Romans, who saw a wife as the property of her husband. In *Gallic War Book VI*, Julius Caesar famously said that Celtic men had the power of life and death over their wives; however, women also enjoyed many legal protections (Green, 1997). For example, they could not be married against their will. Although women may have been allowed to choose their husbands, their families were always involved in the decision, as political alliances through marriage were common among the Celtic nobility. Within marriages, women were also allowed to inherit property independently, and they could be involved in legal cases without the consent of their husbands.

Dowry systems are also suggestive of the relative equality between the sexes in Celtic society. Although practices varied among different Celtic groups, one common custom was for each party to bring an equal sum to the marriage, and the combined amount was put aside to amass profit. When one partner died, the other would receive his or her original share and the profits. This convention seems to have existed in some form among Celtic groups in Wales, Ireland, Gaul (modern-day France), and other parts of Europe.

Also, divorce was simple and could happen at the request of either party. As Celtic marriage was contractual rather than religious, and it was based on the freedom of husband and wife, dissolving it had fewer consequences than would have been the case if it were a faith-based institution (Markale, 1986). A custom of one-year trial marriages that could be ended if they proved impractical existed in Scotland and Ireland. Additionally, divorced women were not looked down on and were always free to remarry if they chose to do so.

What to Expect From This Book

If you're tired of the lack of recognition and invisibility of women in history, this book brings to light the true stories of the female heroes of the Celtic era. If you are interested in female empowerment, you will love reading these accounts of women in history and mythology whose achievements are not widely known.

Chapter 1: Warrior Queens: Bravery Beyond Bounds

This chapter examines the lives of the British queen Boudica, who led a rebellion against Rome, and the mythological Queen Medb of Connacht who stars in the *Ulster Cycle* of Irish mythology and starts a war with Ulster.

Chapter 2: Women Warriors and Peacemakers

The second chapter looks at the career of Cartimandua, the Queen of the Brigantes, and her diplomatic rule as she negotiated power with the Romans. It also considers the legends of the mythological figures of Scáthach, Aífe, and Liath Luachra.

Chapter 3: Priestesses: Spiritual Leadership

The third chapter discusses the role of priestesses in Celtic spirituality, exploring the examples of mythological and historical Celtic women such as Brigid the Bright, Ganna, and Veleda and what their lives tell us about the spiritual world of the Celts.

Chapter 4: Wise Women: Healers, Seers, Poets

This chapter explores traditional Celtic healing practices and the role of wise women. It also covers attitudes toward death and the afterlife and prophecies and predictions. Here, we consider the examples of women such as Macha Mong Ruad, the first woman monarch of Ireland, and Fedelm, the prophetess poet.

Chapter 5: Powerful Female Figures in Celtic Mythology

The penultimate chapter evaluates the lives of several mythological figures, namely Rhiannon, the goddess of sovereignty, The Morrígan, the goddess of war and fate, Ceridwen, the goddess of poetry, magic, and transformation, and Deirdre of the Sorrows.

The concluding section then wraps up everything we have learned in this book. In coming to the end of the book, you will have learned that the Celtic world was full of courageous female leaders. You will have discovered that the Celts were a society that empowered women, one that respected and feared women in many areas, including leadership. For these reasons, this ancient civilization set down the early roots of gender equality, and its legacy is modern-day women's rights advocacy.

Can we learn from this today? If so, could modern women become more empowered than we already are? Read on to find out more...

Chapter Two
Warrior Queens

Bravery Beyond Bounds

While about the shore of Mona those Neronian legoionares
Burnt and broke the grove and altar
of the Druid and Druidesses,
Far in the East Boadicea,
standing loftily charioted,
Mad and Maddening all that heard her
in her fierce volubility,
Girt by half the tribes of Britain,
near the colony Camulodune,
Yell'd and shriek'd between her daughters
o'er a wild confederacy.

– Alfred, Lord Tennyson,
from "Boadicea"

This chapter explores the lives of Celtic warrior queens, both real and mythological. Below, we look at two specific examples: Boudica, the queen of the Iceni, who led a brief rebellion against the Romans in the first century C.E., and Medb, the mythological Queen of Connacht, a key figure in the *Ulster Cycle* of Irish myth.

Boudica: Leader of a Rebellion Against Rome

Boudica, possibly the most famous of the powerful women studied in this book and known also as the Warrior Queen, was a royal lady and a member of the Iceni, an East Anglian tribe. She became their queen in 60/61 C.E., the same year in which she led an uprising of her people and surrounding tribes against the occupying forces of the Roman Empire, a feat she is remembered for today. Below, we look at her leadership, achievements, legacy, and what her life tells us about gender equality within Celtic society.

Accounts of Boudica and Her Uprising

We know of Boudica's life and the uprising she led against the Romans through four classical sources written by three Roman historians. These are the *Agricola* (ca. 98 C.E.) and the *Annals* (ca. 110 C.E.) by Tacitus, a brief record of the uprising recorded by Suetonius in his *Lives of the Caesars* (121 C.E.), and Dio Cassius's history of the Empire, *Romaika* (ca. 202 to ca. 235 C.E.), the longest account of Boudica's life and rebellion against the Romans.

There are reasons why all these texts may not offer entirely accurate accounts of the queen and her revolt. The most reliable of these is likely to be the works of Tacitus. Although he wrote many years after the events, he was the son-in-law of Gnaeus Julius Agricola, who served as a tribune under Suetonius Paulinus at the time of the uprising, so the author of the *Agricola* and the *Annals* likely received a first-hand account (Hingley & Unwin, 2005).

Dio Cassius, on the other hand, began his history of Rome and its empire around 140 years after Boudica's death. Most of what he wrote has been lost, and his account of the queen only survives in the epitome of an 11th-century Byzantine monk, John Xiphilinus. While Dio provides greater and more lurid detail than Tacitus, his embellishments are likely fiction (Grant, 1995).

Both Tacitus and Dio give accounts of Boudica's battle speeches, though her words were never recorded during her lifetime, so these are most likely imaginary (Hingley & Unwin, 2005). These battle speeches were written to present the Romans as morally superior to their enemy. However, this tactic backfired, and, to later generations, Boudica became the patriotic symbol of Britain, and her rebellion has been celebrated ever since.

Background and Early Life

In the Brythonic language, Boudica's name, which can also be spelled Boudicca, comes from the word *boudi*, which means "victory" or "win," that is, "victorious woman." In Latin, her name is written as Boadicea or Boudicea.

Her people, the Iceni, inhabited what is now the English county of Norfolk and parts of the neighboring counties of Cambridgeshire, Suffolk, and Lincolnshire. The tribe is known for having produced some of the earliest British coins (Davies, 2008). According to some sources, the queen's mother was a female Druidess, also known as a *Banduri* (Klimczak, 2016). However, there is no evidence to back up this claim.

Not much is known about the Warrior Queen's early life. In his *Agricola*, Tacitus says that she was of royal birth, describing her as *"generis regii femina"* ("a woman of the royal house" or "a lady of royal descent") while Dio Cassius similarly says that she was "a British woman of the royal family" (Fraser, 1988). However, from these descriptions, it is unclear whether Boudica belonged to the Iceni royal family or another noble lineage. It could be that she was a princess from a neighboring tribe.

Some have speculated that she came from the Brigantes and was related to the other great Celtic queen of that era, Cartimandua. There is no evidence whatsoever to support this romantic notion, however. Another story is that Boudica came from Ireland, a proposal supported by similar torcs being found in Norfolk and Ireland. Again, this "evidence" is not enough to prove that she did come from the neighboring land. Most likely, given the preference for matrilineal inheritance in the Celtic world, she simply belonged to the Iceni royal family (Fraser, 1988).

In 60 C.E., Boudica must have been at least 30 years of age, as she had two living daughters who had reached the age of puberty but were also not yet married and needed their mother's regency. It is likely that these girls were in their early to mid-teens in that year, so they would have been born sometime around 45 to 46 C.E. Boudica would then have been born around 26 to 30 C.E., or she could have been quite a bit older and born earlier. If these two daughters were the youngest survivors of a large family, she may have been 40 years old or older (Fraser, 1988).

Dio Cassius described the famous queen's appearance, saying that she had a mass of "the tawniest [brownish-orange] hair" hanging down to her waist, that she was very tall, and "in appearance almost terrifying" with a fierce expression and a noticeably harsh voice (Fraser, 1988). The Romans described many other Celtic warrior women in similar terms, with many of them describing these women as tall and fearsome. One example is Diodorus Siculus, who described Gaulish women as being extremely brave and tall, while Ammianus Marcellinus commented on their fighting skills (Watts, 2005). These examples suggest that Dio's description of Boudica may be based on his perceptions of Celtic women rather than any surviving eyewitness accounts.

The Iceni had originally revolted against Rome in 47 C.E. when the Roman governor Publius Ostorius Scapula planned to subdue all the people of Britain under the control of the Romans. Once the tribe's uprising was suppressed, the invaders allowed the kingdom to retain its independence (Davies, 2008). From this point onward, Prasutagus, Boudica's husband

and king of the Iceni at the time, entered into a reciprocal contract with Emperor Nero. This meant that his kingdom remained intact and, in exchange, Prasutagus kept the peace and allowed his domain to act as a buffer state (Green, 1997).

Queenship and Rebellion

On his death in 60/61 C.E., Prasutagus made his two daughters and Emperor Nero his heirs (Potter, 2004). After he died, Boudica took over her husband's rule, as their daughters were still minors and too young to reign themselves. The Romans challenged her assumption of power, claiming that she had done so illegally, and they retaliated by confiscating Icenian assets. The desire to ensure that Boudica did not come to power may have been motivated by the Roman view that men under the control of a woman were disgraced and could only regain their dignity by conquering her territories (Green, 1997; McCoppin, 2022).

The Romans also ignored Prasutagus's will, which stated that his daughters were his heirs. Instead, they absorbed the Iceni kingdom into the province of Britannia, sending the procurator of Britain, Catus Decianus, to secure the Iceni kingdom for Rome (Elliott, 2021; Davies, 2008). According to Tacitus, the Romans did more than just take charge of Boudica's dominion. They also punished her for assuming power by raiding the surrounding countryside, ransacking her household, flogging her and her daughters, and also raping the girls (Elliott, 2021).

The public beating of Boudica and her daughters, as well as the additional rape of the young women, drove the queen to seek revenge against the Romans. The enraged woman gathered a huge force of British freedom fighters, including the Iceni's neighbors, the Trinovantes, who also had problems with the Romans. The combined forces totaled 120,000 men (230,000, according to Dio), who were aided by the support of Andraste, the goddess of victory, whom Dio claimed Boudica had called on to support her cause (Green, 1997; Hingley & Unwin, 2005; Potter, 2004).

The queen and her army caused a great deal of destruction in a short space of time. They sacked three major Roman towns, Londinium, Camulodunum, and Verulamium (modern-day London, Colchester, and St Albans, respectively), thereby nearly driving the invaders out of Britain (Green, 1997).

Boudica's forces first struck at Camulodunum (modern-day Colchester), which was then a Roman *colonia* for retired soldiers. There, a temple had been erected to honor Emperor Claudius at the expense of the local population. This, and the mistreatment of the locals by the veterans, had led to much resentment toward the Romans (Webster, 1978; Hingley & Unwin, 2005). After Boudica's rebel army captured the town, the inhabitants who survived the initial attack sought refuge in the Temple of Claudius for two days before they were surrounded and killed.

The Romans suffered such an overwhelming defeat because they had been taken by surprise. This is apparent from their failure to draw their forces behind defenses and to send women, children, and the elderly to a place of safety for the duration of the conflict (Webster, 1978).

Another issue for the Romans was that there were not enough active military forces close to Camulodunum at the time of the revolt to suppress it. The governor of Britain, Gaius Suetonius Paulinus (known to history as Suetonius) was leading a campaign against the island of Mona, off the coast of North Wales (Hingley & Unwin, 2005). The only troops immediately available to help were 200 soldiers based in Londininium, all of whom were too old for active duty and had been put in charge of civil matters, such as protecting property and distributing messages. Although they were still on the official list, Tacitus says that they were not fully equipped to deal with a large rebel army (Webster, 1978).

Eventually, Roman forces under the command of Quintus Petillius Cerialis, who was in charge of Legio IX *Hispana,* tried to relieve Camulodunum but were overwhelmed by the rebels. His infantry forces were all killed, and only the commander and some of his cavalry escaped. This defeat was disastrous, and, soon after, Catus Decianus, whose conduct had provoked the rebellion, fled to Gaul (Highley & Unwin, 2005).

Having sacked this town, Boudica's army then advanced on Londinium. When Suetonius heard of the uprising, he immediately left a garrison on Mona and returned to England to deal with the Warrior Queen. Quickly moving through hostile territory, the Roman governor reached modern-day London before the rebel forces could (Hingley & Unwin, 2005; Webster, 1978). However, it was soon apparent that Suetonius's army was outnumbered, so he decided to abandon the town. The advancing army burned it down and tortured and killed all remaining civilians. They then sacked the municipium of Verulamium (modern-day St Albans), north-west of London (Vandrei, 2018). The extent to which the rebel army destroyed the town is unclear.

Later Classical accounts by Tacitus and Dio report that Boudica's army killed around 80,000 people (Hingley & Unwin, 2005). Tacitus added that the Britons had no interest in taking Roman captives prisoner; instead, they slaughtered them by "gibbet, fire, or cross" (Cunliffe, 1978: 143). Dio added embellishment to this by stating that Roman noblewomen were impaled on spikes and had their breasts cut off and sewn to their mouths during sacrifices, banquets, and other "wanton behavior" in sacred places, particularly the groves of the goddess Andraste (Henshell, 2008: 55). Such accounts are indicative of the rage and resentment that drove the rebel campaign.

Dio lamented: "Moreover, all this ruin was brought upon the Romans by a woman, a fact which in itself caused the greatest shame" (Hingley & Unwin, 2005: 53). Despite their initial defeats, the invader forces quickly regrouped and recovered from their losses. Suetonius raised an army of almost 10,000 men and took a stand in a narrow pass or gorge with woods behind it. The exact location of the defense has never been identified, but the Romans used their position to their advantage, launching javelins at Boudica's army before advancing in a wedge-shaped formation and attacking the rebel forces with their cavalry (Davies, 2008). The Roman army remained heavily outnumbered, but the tactics they had employed worked to their advantage, and Boudica's army was finally defeated. In the aftermath, Tacitus says that neither women nor animals were spared.

He adds that the queen poisoned herself, and Dio states that she fell sick and died, after which she was given a lavish burial. While, on first reading, the Classical accounts contradict each other, Vandrei (2018) suggests that they are not mutually exclusive. Both Tacitus and Dio say that Boudica died shortly after the defeat of her army, either by suicide or because of illness. Possibly, her health had been weakened by campaigning and her brutal treatment at the hands of the Romans months before.

Leadership

Historians acknowledge that Boudica's leadership had ritualistic or holy elements. Frenee-Hutchins (2014) notes that her rebellion had elements of the former, while Antonia Fraser (1988) suggests the Boudica assumed the role of "Holy (Armed) Figurehead," demanding bloody revenge for her people and her daughters.

Boudica's understanding of leadership may have been informed by how queens, who were commonplace in Celtic myth and legend, were portrayed in her culture (Jackson, 1990). The Celts believed that the Iceni ruler and queens like her were directly connected to the conception of divinity. As a queen, they believed that Boudica was connected to the goddess Andraste, the Iceni goddess of war and victory, whom Boudica evoked during her revolt against the Romans (Scholarly Community Encyclopedia, 2024). Dio tells us that this took place as the rebel leader released a hare from her gown during a speech made before one of her battles:

> "Let us, therefore, go against [the Romans], trusting boldly to good fortune. Let us show them that they are hares and foxes trying to rule over dogs and wolves." When she [Boudica] had finished speaking, she employed a species of divination, letting a hare escape from the fold of her dress; and since it ran on what they considered the auspicious side, the whole multitude shouted with pleasure, and Boudica, raising her hand toward heaven, said: "I thank you, Andraste, and call upon you as woman speaking to woman ... I beg you for victory and preservation of liberty."
>
> Hingley & Unwin, 2005: 55

Her intention in releasing the creature from her dress was to make predictions about the outcome of the battle from the direction in which it ran. This was a common Celtic divination technique, similar to Roman methods, in which case they believed that there was a meaning to the direction in which birds flew. Going to the right was thought to bring favor and to the left was the opposite (Fowler, 2020).

Furthermore, according to Dio, Boudica's forces celebrated their victory over the Romans by undertaking sacrifices and feasting in the groves of Andraste (Henshall, 2008). Historians thought that through this, Boudica was able to serve as high priestess to Andraste, giving her semi-divine status. McCoppin (2022) argues that Boudica's high social standing is directly aligned with her people's acceptance of powerful goddesses, as when these divinities are worshipped in cultures, women can occupy and maintain powerful positions. It therefore appears that the Iceni queen assumed the Celtic role of war queen-goddess, just as Queen Medb did in t*he Ulster Cycle* (Frenee-Hutchins, 2014).

Knowledge of Boudica's leadership has been informed by how she was presented by Classical writers and, in her lifetime, by how the Romans saw her as a female leader. However, as we've already established, the Romans had a different view of women and did not believe they had the right to rule.

The rebellion initially came about because the Romans had claimed her lands and physically punished her and her daughters by public thrashing. Her daughters were also raped, and she was forced to watch (McCoppin, 2022). This act against her children had divine and political significance, as explained below:

> As co-heirs of their mother, the girls shared the divinity that was attached to her. Rape robbed them of their supernatural abilities and debarred them from claiming priestess status or inheriting her semi-divine role, breaking the "mother right" of matrilineal descent.
> Cross & Miles, 2011: 32

This act demonstrates how Boudica's power was derived from her divine status. By raping her daughters, the Romans hoped to destroy their (and by extension, Boudica's) power in the eyes of the Celts.

Sadly, rape and other crimes against women are still used today as revenge for the actions of conquering armies. Instances of such abhorrent behavior were recorded during the Second World War and remain prevalent in conflict situations today.

Legacy

Boudica lives on as a symbol of the strength Celtic women were sometimes allowed to display in their communities. At present, the Warrior Queen is enjoying a national resurgence in Britain as a symbol of rebellion and the fight against oppression as well as a figure women can aspire to (Barnett, 2023).

From a historical viewpoint, it is uncertain whether the Classical accounts of her rebellion are entirely accurate, and it is a pity that she was never given the chance to tell her own story. According to Elizabeth Cleone Hopland, a Colchester-based actor and director who has portrayed Boudica on stage:

> She is most definitely relevant today. She is a beacon of strength for many. Women are still getting taken advantage of; we need women to feel safe in our communities and that they feel they are heard. Boudicca represents the power of the women scorned.
>
> Barnett, 2023

Thus, Boudica was an example of a fearsome Celtic warrior queen who refused to be oppressed by the Roman forces and, because of that, is an ongoing inspiration for women. Today, Boudica is a familiar presence in popular culture. In London, there is a statue of her that can be found on the Victoria Embankment next to Westminster Bridge, where it has stood since 1902 (Hingley & Unwin, 2006). She has also entered popular culture, appearing in films and musicals, such as the film *Boudica* (2023) and the musical of the same title that was performed at Shakespeare's Globe Theatre in 2017. She has also appeared in artworks.

Medb: Queen of Connacht

Introduction

One of the most vibrant female personalities to come out of Celtic myth and legend was Medb, also known as Meadbh, Maeve, and Maev. She was the queen of Connacht and is one of the key figures in the *Ulster Cycle*. She is depicted in those myths as an independent ruler, as the commander of armies, and as more important than any of her many consorts (Green, 1997; MacKillop, 1998).

Once thought to have been a historical figure, Medb is now believed to be a combination of several goddesses. She incorporates the qualities of the goddesses of territory, fertility, and sovereignty, and her character may owe something to the territorial goddess Mór Muman of Munster, who is associated with the powers of the sun and sovereignty (MacKilliop, 1998).

Medieval scribes gave the queen a detailed biography. According to them, her father was Eochaid Feidlech, one of the most important pre-Christian kings of Tara, and her mother is sometimes named Crucha, for whom the fortress of Cruachan was named. Among her brothers was Finn Emna, while her sisters were Clothra, Eithne, and Mugain. Medb also had at least four husbands, eight sons, three daughters, two children by a lover, and an adopted son (MacKillop, 1998).

Descriptions of the queen follow literary conventions. She is said to have been pale and long faced with flowing hair. She wore a red cloak and carried a spear that may have been on fire. She was able to run as fast as any horse, and the sight of her could deprive men of two-thirds of their strength. She also did not seem to age and was reported to have the allure of a beautiful young woman regardless of chronology (MacKillop, 1998). Thus, Medb was both a beauty and as fearsome as any real-life Celtic warrior woman.

Key Events and Achievements

Medb was immortalized by four texts from the *Ulster Cycle*. These are:

- "Táin Bó Cúailnge" ("Cattle Raid of Cooley")
- "Fled Bricrenn" ("Briccriu's Feast")
- "Echtra Nerai" ("The Adeventure of Nera")
- "Scéla Mucce Meic Da Thó" ("The Story of Mac Da Thó's Pig")

Medb is a strident supporting player in the latter three texts, but in "The Táin," she leads the action. In this tale, she demonstrates more conviction than her husband, Ailill mac Máta. She is a woman of action, leading the Connacht forces and providing the central drama of the narrative (MacKillop, 1998).

One of her main achievements was becoming queen of Connacht in her own right and wielding power in her role. The story of how Medb came to power and married her third husband, Ailill mac Máta, is told in "Cath Boinde," or "The Battle of the Boyne" in English, also known as "Ferchuitred Medba," or "Medb's Man-Share". The story begins with her first marriage to Conchobar mac Nessa, whom her father married her to because he had killed the man thought to be Conchobar's father, the former High King Fachtna Fáthach, in battle (Depuis, 2009). The couple had a son, Glaisne, but the marriage was unhappy, and Medb left her first husband.

One story says that to compensate Medb former husband, her father, Eochaid Feidlech, arranged for Medb's sister, Clothra, to marry Conchobar and left instructions for her to be made queen of Connacht. Medb was furious, killed her pregnant sister, and took the crown by force (Depuis, 2009). Another story claims that after she left Conchobar, Eochaid deposed Tinni mac Conri, the then-king of Connacht, and installed Medb as queen instead so that she could have a kingdom of her own (Williamson & McMenemy, 2023). Tinni regained part of his lost throne when he and Medb became lovers and married.

What happened next is undisputed. Conchobar raped Medb (some say in retaliation for killing Clothra, his wife and her sister), and a war between Ulster and Connacht ensued. Some say Eochaid began the war in his outrage over the rape of his daughter. During the conflict, Conchobar is said to have killed Eochaid (Heinz, 1997). Other versions of the story say that Tinni mac Conri challenged Conchobar to single combat and lost (MacKillop, 1998).

During this war one man named Eochaid Dala proved to be such a loyal subject to Medb, saving her from Conchobar and bringing her to Connacht, that she took him as her husband and made him the new king of Connacht on the condition that he was not to be miserly, apprehensive, or jealous so as not to dishonor her (Depuis, 2009; Heinz, 1997).

When she married Dala, she also hired 17-year-old Ailill mac Máta as her royal bodyguard, and he soon became her lover. After he defeated Eochaid in single combat, she wedded her young subject under the Brehon marriage contract, also known as the *Lánamnas fir for bantinacur*, which applies to unions where the man brings less property to the marriage than the woman. This indicates that Medb was the dominant party of the pair, which is unsurprising since Ailill had been appointed to serve and protect her (Depuis, 2009).

Perhaps the most famous event Medb is associated with is the narrative of "The Táin" (the "Cattle Raid of Cooley"). This narrative records conflicts involving the kingdom of Ulster in some unidentified past, considered to be around the time of Christ, so the early first century C.E. The hero of the story is Cú Chulainn, a Superman-like figure and an inspiration for the heroes of modern-day fantasy literature.

The story opens with Medb calculating the sum of her belongings and those of Ailill. She discovers that he had one powerful stud bull more than she did, making her the less equal of the pair. To rectify this, she finds a better bull in Ulster that is owned by Dáire mac Fiachna. When he refuses to sell it to her, she declares war, enlisting the help of her army and her lover, Fergus mac Róich, to secure the bull for herself (Depuis, 2009). Medb is not put off by a prophecy of impending doom, so her army proceeds to Ulster (Britannica, 2024a).

As this kingdom was under a divine curse at that time, the only warrior left to fight against the Connacht invaders was the young Cú Chulainn, who demanded single combat. Medb offers her daughter Findabair in marriage to a series of warriors as payment for fighting the hero, but they are all defeated. The conflict climaxes in a three-day combat between the exiled Cú Chulainn and Ferdiad, his friend and foster brother, and Medb's forces. Although he nearly dies from wounds and exhaustion, the warrior is victorious. The Ulster army then joins him and defeats the Connacht warriors. Despite losing the war with Ulster, Medb secures the bull, which then fights Ailill's stud, but both creatures die as a result (Britannica, 2024; Depuis, 2009).

One interesting feature of "The Táin" is that it depicts Medb as a petty woman who is obsessed with being more powerful than her husband. This leads her into a war that she loses. The outcome of both her and her husband's bulls perishing when she does obtain her desired prize suggests that there is something unnatural and destructive about a husband and wife fighting to be more powerful than each other.

The Irish legend also depicts Medb as a usurper of the masculine role. To this end, the narrative judges her by "traditional criteria for the male role she aspires for" (Kelly, 1992: 81). Therefore, she is condemned for failing to fulfill the role of a successful king and victorious military leader. However, Lehmann (2008) proposes that despite overt the tale's criticism and demonization of her character, it also emphasizes the internal strength of Medb's character. As such, "The Táin" highlights her power as a woman and how this allows her to become a fearsome leader in her own right.

Marriage, Motherhood, and Sexuality

The order and total number of Medb's husbands are uncertain, although four have been named in various sources. MacKillop (1998) thinks that Conchobar mac Nessa was her first and states that it was "pride of mind" that led her to leave his company. Later on, he would become her great enemy. However, Conchobar still lusted after his former wife and later violated her while she was bathing in the Boyne. At one time or another, all of her three sisters were also married to the man. That Medb killed her sister Clothra while she was pregnant with Conchobar's child was a treacherous act that would eventually lead to her death.

Medb's three other husbands all successively became kings of Connacht. They were Tinni mac Conri, who Conchobar killed, Eochaid Dala, her least well-known husband who only became king because she consented to have him as a husband, and Ailill mac Máta, her best-known husband and a mere boy at the time of their marriage. One telling suggests that a "water-worm" that eventually became Finnbennach, the White Bull of Connacht led Medb to Ailill (MacKillop, 1998).

The account of Medb's death comes from an 11th-century story written long after the events of "The Táin" (MacKillop, 1998). It may be the case that Medieval Christian scribes felt that she could not get away with what they perceived to be immoral behavior, seeing as in their accounts, her complicated love life is what ultimately leads to her death.

After Medb killed her sister Clothra during her pregnancy with Conchobar's child, the infant was cut from the dying woman's womb. The baby survived and grew up to be Furbaide Ferbend, who lived on an island in Lough Ree, County Roscommon that Medb also went to live on. There, she went bathing each morning. One day, as she had her daily swim, Furbaide discovered that she was his mother's killer. In response, he took a hardened piece of cheese that he had been eating, placed it in his sling, and shot it, hitting the queen squarely on the head and killing her.

Medb is depicted as an extremely sexual person. She has been said to have boasted that she "was never without one man being with [her] in the shadow of another" (Watts, 2005: 14). Many men were named as her lovers, but Fergus mac Róich was her favorite. Sources state she said that it took either 32 men or Fergus alone to satisfy her sexually (MacKillop, 1998; Meyer, 1897).

The relationship between Medb and this lover is a subplot of "The Táin" and is also hinted at in the early poem "Conailla Medb Míchuru" ("Medb Has Entered Evil Contracts") by Luccreth moccu Chíara (ca. 600). This text tells how she accidentally seduced Fergus into turning against Ulster "because he preferred the buttocks of a woman to his own people" (Tristram, 1998).

The infamous Queen of Connacht's sexual activity is also often discussed and alluded to in myths. For example, "The Táin" opens with Medb's bickering pillow talk with Ailill, with the couple arguing over who owns the greatest bull. Her adultery with Fergus also continues throughout the narrative, and, at one point, her husband catches them having sex. Ailill eventually gets his revenge, arranging for Fergus to be speared while the lovers are swimming (MacKillop, 1998). These examples show how Medb's sexuality was a prominent part of her character and was an integral part of her power.

Medb had numerous children. We've already mentioned Glaisne, her son with Conchobar mac Nessa. She also had at least three daughters. The best-known was Finnabair, whom many stories were written about, and the others were Cainder and Faife. Medb had two children with Fergus mac Róich, who gave their names to the land: Ciar is the eponym of Ciarri (Kerry) while Conmac is the eponym of Conmaiene Mara (Connemara). She gave the name "Maine" to all of the seven sons she had with Ailill mac Máta due to a misreading of a Druidic prophecy that a son of that name would kill Conchobar. Finally, Medb adopted another son, Etarcomul.

Medb's maternal nature is symbolized by how, like a Gaulish mother-goddess, she is often portrayed with creatures such as a bird or a squirrel on her shoulder (MacKillop, 1998).

Legacy

The example of Queen Medb suggests that the idea of strong women was widely accepted in the Celtic world (O'Hara, 2023). However, the plot of "The Táin" suggests that Medieval writers may have seen her powerful position as unnatural and, thus, sought to present her as selfish and self-centered. Nevertheless, she comes across as a mighty, independent woman who made her own decisions rather than letting men make them on her behalf.

Interpretations of Medb's character and actions have been informed by beliefs concerning the meaning of her name. Since the late 18th century, scholars have thought that her name relates to the Old Irish words *medb* meaning "strong, intoxicating [of alcoholic beverages]" and *mid*, translating to "mead" (Irslinger, 2013). This belief was applied to interpret her character and behavior in "The Táin."

Pinault (2007) questioned the association between Medb and mead when he proposed that her name related to several similar Gaulish names, all of which came from the Indo-European *med* ("to govern"). This discovery indicates that, for the Celts, Medb was an example of a female leader rather than a mediator, as previously believed.

Some sources have proposed that Medb was the goddess who bestowed sovereignty on kings during the ritual of *hieros gamas* (the "sacred marriage"). This comprised the draught of mead and involved the ruler marrying the local fertility goddess to secure his sovereignty (Irslinger, 2013). This ritual also emphasizes the power that female deities were associated with in the Celtic world, as for monarchs to receive their status, a divinity who had a direct connection to the prosperity of the land had to sanctify their coronation. This process required a sexual encounter between the king and a priestess, who played the role of the divine being so that the new ruler could serve as the figurehead for the virility of the land (McCoppin, 2022; Sullivan, 2024).

The sacred marriage ritual also demonstrates the role of women as mediators of power in the Celtic world. Notably, Plutarch refers to a long-standing tradition of Celtic women acting in this role in military and political disputes.

Summary

The real-life example of Queen Boudica and the legend of Queen Medb demonstrate the powerful roles Celtic women could play in their society. Historians and other commentators have had difficulty understanding and appreciating these fierce female warriors, as they show that women are more than passive victims of brutality but are individuals capable of inflicting violence upon others. Despite this, their examples also show how much freedom women in this society enjoyed compared to their Classical counterparts. For this reason, both figures remain inspirations for women today.

The next chapter looks at the dual role of Celtic warrior queens as combatants and peacemakers, considering how feminine power could be combined with more divine qualities.

Chapter Three
Women Warriors and Peacemakers

The women of the Gauls are not only like men in their great stature, but they are a match for them in courage as well.
— Diodorus Siculus

IN THIS CHAPTER, WE look at the lives of even more Celtic women warriors and peacemakers. Below, we explore the examples of Cartimandua, Queen of the Brigantes, who famously made peace with the Romans and gave her people 26 years of stable rule. We also look at female warriors from Celtic myth, namely rival warrior queens (also sometimes said to be sisters) Scáthach and Aífe. Finally, we discuss Liath Luachra, one of the foster mothers and instructors of the hero Fionn mac Cumhaill. These examples emphasize the diverse roles warrior women played in Celtic society.

Cartimandua: Diplomat Queen

Background

Cartimandua (meaning "pony" or "small horse") was the first-century C.E. queen of the Brigantes, a Celtic people living in what is now northern England, close to the Scottish border (Lewis, 2017). The queen ruled over a loose conglomeration of Brigantian tribes from around 43 to 69 C.E. For her to be accepted by these diverse factions, she would have likely been a member of one of their leading families. Her position was strengthened politically by a dynastic marriage to Venutius, who came from one of the tribes from the territory to the north (Webster, 1993).

Cartimandua reigned during the period that the Romans began their conquest of Britain. Her queenship is notable for her alliance with the invaders, in contrast to many of her fellow Britons, such as Boudica, whom we met in the previous chapter, who rebelled against Roman rule.

Tacitus composed his accounts of the Brigantes and Cartimandua's rule in his *Histories* and his *Annals*, composed later but dealing with events that took place during the reigns of Emperors Claudius and Nero, and he positioned them under the year 69 C.E. According to him, Cartimandua was of "illustrious birth," suggesting that she inherited her position through matrilineal descent rather than acquiring her queenship through marriage (Pennington, 2003). Although no physical description of her survives, the historian describes her as a glamorous, powerful figure "flourishing in all the splendor of wealth and power" (Lewis, 2017).

The center of Cartimandua's rule has been suggested to be an earthwork complex at Stanwick, North Yorkshire in northern England. During her reign, the town expanded to occupy an area of 1.2 miles, and regular deliveries of Roman goods such as wine, rare tableware, glass, and amphorae (pottery containers) were dropped off at the settlement. These incoming goods indicate that the queen's domains enjoyed a close connection and favor with the Roman Empire. It is also apparent that neighboring locations, such as Scotch Corner, also benefitted from the regular supplies of Roman goods, and they produced raw materials for manufacturing (Roberts, 2024). Based on this, Stanwick seems to have been a long-term base for Cartimandua and her subjects.

Archaeological excavations suggest that the complex was not densely occupied. Its walls were impressive in height in certain places but offered a limited defense against a disciplined army. This indicates that it was not a permanent town or stronghold, although it may have been used to host important gatherings (Roberts, 2024).

The site was first excavated by Sir Mortimer Wheeler from 1951–1952 and later between 1981 and 2009 under Colin Haselgrove. Wheeler originally believed that it was the center of Venutius's independent rule after Cartimandua's defeat, but opinion now favors the above-mentioned conclusion that it had been the queen's base (Lewis, 2017). This is evidenced by an archaeological analysis that revealed that there had been a flood of imported goods deposited and used at the site between 40 and 70 C.E., roughly around the time of the queen's reign and the period when she ruled as a Roman client (Symonds, 2017). This is in alignment with what we know about her close collaboration with the Empire and her rule abruptly ending in 69 C.E.

Loyalty to Rome

One of the things that Cartimandua is known for is her loyalty to Rome and her desire to keep peace with them. In contrast to some of her well-known contemporary Britons, such as Boudica and Caratacus, Cartimandua did not rebel against Roman rule. The Brigantes did not join the Warrior Queen's rebellion in 60/61 C.E., probably due to their ruler's policy of keeping the peace with the Romans (Lewis, 2017).

In the mid-first century C.E., the Romans were in the process of conquering Britain. Realizing that she was unlikely to halt their progress, the queen and her husband decided to make peace with the invaders instead of challenging them. In exchange, she was allowed to continue to rule over her people as a client queen, creating an arrangement desirable to the Empire. Namely, they gained a dependable ruler with hegemony over the diverse northern tribes (Lewis, 2017; Snyder, 2003). Cartimandua, for her part, maintained her allegiance because the conquerors had helped her to consolidate her power in northern Britain.

The most famous example of her loyalty is how she handed over the chained rebel leader, Caratacus, to the Romans after the Catuvellauni chieftain sought sanctuary with her following his defeat by Ostorius Scapula in Wales in 51 C.E. In the decade before, the rebel had made himself the leader of the early British resistance against the Empire's rule. In 48 C.E., his forces attacked the Roman armies as they moved forward to conquer what is now Wales. The invaders eventually held off the attack, leading the rebels to seek protection from Cartimandua (Lewis, 2017).

Tacitus records that the Brigantes queen betrayed the chieftain because he had sought refuge in her territories, so she instead sent him to Rome (Birley, 1980). He notes that the Romans rewarded her loyalty with great wealth, indicating that the alliance was profitable to Cartimandua and provided her and her kingdom protection and military backup when they needed it.

There has been some suggestion that there was a familial link between Cartimandua and Caratacus. Welsh legend says that they were second cousins while the Scots believed that the queen was his stepmother (Howarth, 2008). There could have been a link between the two through intermarriage between the Brigantes and Catuvellauni tribes, but there is no evidence to prove it.

There has been similar speculation that Boudica was a member of the Brigantes royal family and married into the Iceni, which would mean she was a relation of Cartimandua (Fraser, 1988). However, this is nothing more than conjecture, which means there is no known link between the two queens.

Nikki Howarth (2008) suggests that speculation of a connection between the two was put about to make Cartimandua's actions toward him seem like an even greater betrayal. Perhaps such conjecture is rooted in a wider sense of betrayal that Cartimandua, one of the first British women to rule as a queen in her own right, should be more loyal to the Romans than her fellow Britons.

End of Rule

Cartimandua's rule did not go unchallenged. During her reign, she faced a power struggle among the Brigantes and even, at one point, against her husband, Venutius. On these occasions, she asked for help from the Romans. When addressing the conflict with her spouse, it was with the Empire's support that the pair made peace (Lewis, 2017).

However, a later conflict between Cartimandua and Venutius would be her downfall. Around 57 C.E., Cartimandua divorced her husband to begin a relationship with his armor-bearer, Vellocatus. After that point, this is whom she shared her throne and her bed with. (Watts, 2005). Tacitus says that she repudiated her former husband, claiming that she "gave his armor-bearer Vellocatus her hand in marriage. At once her house was convulsed by the scandal. The husband had the state (*civitas*) on his side, the adulterer had the lust and savagery of the queen" (Birley, 1980: 25).

The replaced Brigantes king reacted to being cuckolded by making war against Cartimandua and her Roman protectors. Hostilities began when she took her former brother-in-law and some of his kinsmen prisoner. In response, Venutius sent a band of armed men into her territory. Although he had been married to Cartimandua and Tacitus viewed him as a leader of part of the Brigantes, Venutius seems to have had control over another unnamed territory from where he now sent warriors to invade his former wife's kingdom.

That he was not titled "king" in these accounts suggests that most of his power was derived from his marriage (Hingley, 2022). Tacitus implies that Venutius gained the support of the Brigantes people after Cartimandua left him for Vellocatus; however, further analysis of events suggests that favor for Venutius may not have been so universal.

Thanks to prompt support from Roman forces, Cartimandua resisted the first rebellion; however, when he attacked again in 69 C.E., she was not so fortunate. According to Tacitus, the rebel, aided by surrounding nations, took advantage of the disorder in Rome that had arisen from the Year of the Four Emperors to stage another revolt. Because of the political instability when the Brigantes leader appealed to the Romans for help, they could only supply her with auxiliaries. As a result, she lost control of her territories.

Cartimandua had inherited pre-eminence among her people through her support of Rome. On the other hand, Venutius led another semi-independent people who remained under the overall control of the Brigantes ruler. So, by turning against her, Venutius had also broken his alliance with Rome, leading to his downfall (Hingley, 2022).

Cartimandua and her new husband were eventually taken under the protection of the Romans and removed from her old kingdom. After this, she disappears from history. Within two years of her defeat and exile, the Romans had taken over the Brigantes, overthrown Venutius, and taken direct rule of the kingdom (Birley, 1980; Lewis, 2017).

Legacy

Cartimandua is not generally remembered well by historians, and many scholarly texts present her as a "power-hungry seductress" (Howarth, 2008: 16). Such depictions may be based on negative portrayals of her in the written accounts of Tacitus and in the Welsh Triads, where she is called "Aregwedd Foeddawg." In these texts, she is presented as a deceitful Roman collaborator. For example, in an early Welsh poem, Aregwedd Foeddawg is said to have by "craft and deceit and treachery" placed Caradawc (Caratacus) in Roman hands (Birley, 1980: 25).

Meanwhile, Tacitus describes Cartimandua as "a traitor queen" stating that, "powerful from her nobility, she had increased her power when, by the capture through trickery of the King Caratacus, she appeared to have provided material for the triumph of Claudius Caesar" (Birley, 1980: 25). This act demonstrated her loyalty to Rome and showed how the historian saw her as disloyal to her land for handing over another British leader. According to him, the queen's treacherous act was followed by the "wealth and extravagance that goes with success" (Birley, 1980: 25). This suggests that he blamed Cartimandua's inflated ego for her eventual downfall.

Tacitus mainly presents Cartimandua as part of a discussion of the Tacitean discourse of *libertas*. In this context, she is presented as a negative foil for Boudica. The Roman also depicts the ruler of the Brigantes in strongly gendered terms, juxtaposing the queen's skilled diplomacy with the pride and faithfulness of her ousted husband. Similarly, her new consort, Vellocatus is depicted as falling prey to a power-hungry and oversexed queen (Wilker, 2023).

Cartimandua was the first documented queen to have ruled part of Britain in her own right, yet she is virtually unknown today. This is in direct contrast to her contemporary Boudica, who is celebrated for avenging the cruel treatment of her daughters and her people under a tyrannical regime (Howarth, 2008). Cartimandua, instead, was complicit with the Roman Empire, which may be why history is less favorable to her.

Nevertheless, her story is an important part of the history of Britain, as it demonstrates how women were accepted as leaders and rulers in Celtic cultures. Her story also offers a contrast to that of Boudica, as she remained in power for such a long time because she had been able to negotiate peace and an alliance with the Romans. By way of contrast, the Iceni queen's reign was brief because she rebelled against and refused to submit to Roman rule (Lewis, 2017). Boudica is admired today as a freedom fighter;

however, it could be argued that Cartimandua was the better queen as her alliance with Rome brought prosperity and stability to the Brigantes.

Scáthach: The Shadowy One

Background

Scáthach is an Amazonian female warrior-queen in the type of the early Irish Queen Medb, who appears as a character in the *Ulster Cycle*. Her name is also rendered as Scath, Scáthach nUanaind, or Skatha, meaning "shadow," "shade," "shelter," or "under the protection of" (MacKillop, 1998: 334). Her exploits take place in modern-day Scotland.

Some texts say that she lived in Alpi, which most commentators believe refers to Alba (Scotland). Other texts link her to the Hebridean Isle of Skye, which was called Dunscaith or Dun Sgathaich for her. She was said to reside in a *dun* or fort.

Scáthach had two sons, Cuar and Cet, and a daughter, Uathach, which translates to "specter." (MacKillop, 1998; Wyatt, 2009). She appears to have been entirely independent, as no husband is ever mentioned in the legends surrounding her. In addition, she and her sister Aífe may have been the daughters of Ard-Grimne ("high power") of Lethra, a sun god (Meyer, 1904; Frankel, 2015).

Training School for Young Warriors

Scáthach taught martial arts to Celtic heroes. One of her best-known pupils is Cú Chulainn, who completed his training under her. The tale "Tochmarc Emire" ("The Wooing of Emer") tells of how the hero traveled across the Irish Sea to receive his military training in Scotland. At her fort, Scáthach actively trained her two sons, Cuar and Cet, in the art of war, and she agreed to do the same for Cú Chulainn after he threatened and overcame her by setting his sword between her breasts (Wyatt, 2009).

She furthermore granted the hero three wishes, apparently under duress (Ross, 1970). These were for her to continue to instruct him most carefully, give him her daughter, Uathach, without paying the bride price, and predict his future career. Under her tuition, he mastered his famous aggressive leap, the *torannchless* ("thunder feat"), and also received his spear, the Gáe Bulga. In return, Cú Chulainn aided Scáthach against her enemy (and also her double, sister, or twin), Aífe (MacKillop, 1998).

As part of his instruction, the hero appears to have had a sexual relationship with the warrior-queen. Accounts of Cú Chulainn's amorous adventures with her vary. Usually, he is said to have gained "the friendship of her thighs," which may have been tied to the now-forgotten sexual rite of warrior initiation (MacKillop, 1998). Many scholars believe that among the early Indo-European tribes, educating youths in hunting and warrior skills was part of an initiation process that took place in the context of a homosexual relationship between a student and an adult (male) warrior (Neill, 2009). Scáthach and Cú Chulainn's relationship may echo this custom. Because she is a woman who fills the relevant role, this relationship would still have been acceptable to medieval readers, as the early Christians believed homosexuality to be a mortal sin.

Cú Chulainn also enjoyed intimacies with Scáthach's only daughter, Uathach, whom he later married and who was the one to initiate the relationship. She offered to tell her future husband what he must do to obtain her mother's secrets if he slept with her in return (Markale, 1984).

Scholars view the sexual encounters Cú Chulainn enjoyed with Scáthach, Uathach, and her sister Aífe as the union of the apprentice with his heroic calling rather than evidence that he was a serial womanizer or seducer (MacKillop, 1998). His initiation with women warriors in "Tochmarc Emire" was as much a matter of sexual learning as it was about war. The link between the two was underlined by sexual relations between the "mistress" and the student (Markale, 1984).

The union between Cú Chulainn and Uathach does not exclude or undermine the relationship between the hero and Scáthach. Furthermore, the names of the mother and daughter are significant here, as the young warrior submits to a "terrible" (Uathach) initiation, "which causes fear" (Scáthach). The eventual marriage between the young man and the daughter is an "annual" marriage, an amorous relationship solidified by a legal and temporary contract; meanwhile, relations between the hero and the mother are purely sexual (Markale, 1984: 89).

To fully understand Scáthach and her significance in Celtic myth and legend, it is important to explore the story of her supposed sister, twin, or double, Aífe.

Aífe: Warrior Princess

Background

Aífe, Aoife, or Aiffe, was an Amazonian chieftainess who had a reputation for being "the hardest woman warrior in the world" (MacKillop, 1998: 6). She has also been described as "arrogantly indifferent to the world of men" (Ross, 1970: 210). According to several early Irish narratives, she lived in Alba, and one story says that Aífe was the daughter of Airdgreme.

She was frequently in conflict with Scáthach, who MacKillop (1998) suggests may have been her double. On the other hand, in the story "Aided Óenfhir Aífe" ("The Tragic Death of Aífe's Only Son"), she is said to live in Letha (the Armorican Peninsula in Gaul) and to be the sister or twin, as well as the rival, of the warrior-queen of the previous section, with both being the daughters of Airdgreme of Lethra (Meyer, 1904).

According to accounts, Aífe cared for nothing more than her horses and chariot, and she may have had links with continental goddesses like Epona, who was the Gaulish horse deity (MacKillop, 1998; Green, 1997). The cult of Epona was important to the Celts, as horsepower and horsemanship were vital for the success and survival of the tribe.

Aífe and Cú Chulainn

The best-known story about Aífe, which is told in "Tochmarc Emire," is how Cú Chulainn vanquished her in combat and became her lover (MacKillop, 1998). While he was training with Scáthach, a battle broke out between the instructor and Aífe. Concerned about the warrior's safety, Scáthach gives him a sleeping potion to keep him away from the action. However, what would have put most people to sleep for an entire day only knocked him out for an hour, so he joined the fight (Meyer, 1888).

During the battle, Aífe challenges Scáthach to single combat, but Cú Chulainn fights as his trainer's champion. Before they fight, he asks his tutor what Aífe loves most, and she tells him. The champion and his opponent begin to fight. Aífe gets the advantage by shattering his sword, after which he cries out that her chariot and horses have fallen over a cliff. This is a trick, inspired by the answer he got from Scáthach.

Alarmed, Aífe turns to look. The student then takes the opportunity to overpower her, throwing her over his shoulder, and carrying her back to his side. He holds his sword to her throat, and Aífe begs for her life. Cú Chulainn chooses not to kill her on two conditions. First, that she makes peace with her sister, and second, that she bears him a son (Meyer, 1888).

As was the case with his sexual liaison with Scáthach, Cú Chulainn's coupling with Aífe was part of his apprenticeship to his heroic calling rather than evidence of womanizing (MacKillop, 1998). The sexual union between the two produced a son, Connla. The young hero gave Aífe a gold ring to give to the child and told her to send the boy to Ireland to find his father once he had reached the age of seven; however, the boy was not to identify himself to anyone (Meyer, 1888).

Eventually, Cú Chulainn battled with this son in "Aided Óenfhir Aífe". In this tale, Connla travels to Ireland in search of his father, and his precocious powers alarm the locals. Because he has been instructed not to identify himself, the boy does not reveal his identity to Cú Chulainn, who fights and kills him (Meyer, 1904). It is only after Connla is dead that the hero recognizes the ring, realizing, to his regret, that he has killed his only son (Rolleston, 1986). Aífe's reaction to the death goes unrecorded.

In another version of the story, when Cú Chulainn leaves Scáthach's warrior training school, he goes to fight Aífe. During their struggle, she breaks his sword so that "it was no longer than its hilt" (Wyatt, 2009: 196). The hero then distracts his opponent through trickery, and following this, he abducts her, throws her to the ground, and rapes her. Aífe is impregnated and prophesies that she will give birth to a son. On this occasion, as Scáthach had done, Aífe also grants Cú Chulainn three wishes:

> At that Cuchulind [Cú Chulainn] approached her, seized her under the breast, threw her across (his shoulder) like a burden, and went to his own host ... to throw her on the ground. "Life for life," she said. "My three wishes to me," said he, "Thou shalt have them." "These are my three wishes; thou to give hostages to Scáthach without ever again opposing her, to be with me this night before thy own dun, and to bear me a son."
>
> Wyatt, 2009: 196–197

Following his sexual encounter with Aífe, the warrior departed from her fort never to return, leaving only a name for his unborn child. Wyatt (2009) explains that the defeat of Aífe and her army through forced sexual submission in plain view of her men was alluded to in the tale. This version of "Tochmarc Emire" shows how Cú Chulainn reasserted his warrior prowess by dishonoring and disempowering Aífe. To bring her under his subjection, he applied the ultimate example of masculine physical dominance and violated her sexually.

This version of the story may be a medieval, patriarchal spin on the original, where Aífe is depicted as having more say in the situation. Ross (1970) renders her "arrogant" for being "indifferent" to men, implying that the attempt to assert sexual dominance over her, in theory, is somehow a return to the natural order of things. However, in this day and age, we should question whether Aífe needs a man in her life. After all, she and Scáthach appear to be great examples of empowered, single women who don't need men to feel happy and fulfilled.

For the Celts, figures like these two women and the ultimate warrior-queen, Medb, were examples of the all-powerful goddess. Ross (1970: 211) explains that:

> All of these powerful warrior-goddess queens ... can be thought of as being related in some way to each other, and all may ... represent the concept of the goddess over and above the tribe, the great goddess of the gods themselves.

Thus, Celtic warrior queens represented the ultimate example of physical and divine power.

Liath Luachra: Druidess Warrior

Background

Liath Luachra, also known as Liath Luachair or Lia Luchar meaning "grey of Luchair," is described as a hideous warrior (MacKillop, 1998). She is also referred to as Luaths Lurgann, meaning "speedy foot," which is apt since she was said to be the fastest runner in Ireland (Monaghan, 2004). She is briefly mentioned in the *Fenian Cycle* as a guardian to the young

Fionn mac Cumhaill. She became the "treasurer" of the Fianna after the death of Cumhall, while his killer, Goll mac Morna, was in command. In revenge, Cumhall's son, Fionn mac Cumhaill, killed mac Morna and took his treasures from him (MacKillop, 1998).

The Upbringing of Fionn mac Cumhaill

In "The Boyhood Deeds of Fionn," Liath Luachra raised Fionn mac Cumhaill together with his aunt, the Druidess Bodhmall, who nursed him and began his education after the death of the boy's father. He was originally named "Deimne," but because he grew up to be fair and strong, he was later renamed "Fionn" meaning "fair one" (Eyres, 2007: 263).

Along with the boy's aunt, Liath Luachra is sometimes said to have been the midwife at Fionn's birth (Monaghan, 2004). The women bring him up in secret in the forest of Sliabh Bladhma to protect him from those envious of his great potential. Here, they continue Fionn's education, with Liath training him in martial arts. Alongside Bodhmall, the woman warrior teaches Fionn how to survive on his own until his fame threatens to direct his father's killers to him. After this, they send the boy away for his safety (MacKillop, 1998).

Although Fionn is devoted to Liath Luachra, he accidentally kills her. When an enemy is pursuing Fionn, he picks her up and runs to safety. However, he runs so fast that the wind tears through her body and rips her to shreds, leaving only her thighbones behind. A devastated Fionn uses the remains to dig a lake, which is still known by her name: Loch Lurgainn (Monaghan, 2004).

Liath Luachra is also depicted as the keeper of the crane bag, which becomes one of the greatest treasures of the Fianna, in the *Fenian Cycle* (MacKillop, 1998). The bag had belonged to Fionn's father and held the greatest treasures of the land. It was made from the skin of a crane, which was actually a woman who had been enchanted into the bird's form. This bag is said to symbolize sovereignty, as it had been bestowed on the worthy hero by a goddess (van der Hoeven, 2017). Attempts to gain possession of the crane bag are part of the plot of several hero tales, including that of Fionn mac Cumhaill, and an alternative version of Liath Luachra's death holds that the young Fionn kills her to take the bag for himself (Matson, 2004). This differs from the account mentioned earlier, as it suggests her death is intentional rather than an accident.

The origin of the bag is interesting in itself. One version is that a jealous sorceress called Aoife was turned into a bird after she turned the children of Lir into swans. She flew away to live on the sea, the domain of Manannán mac Lir and, despite her wickedness, she lived to the age of 200 and died from natural causes. After her death, Manannán crafted a bag from her feathery skin. Treasures, such as items of worth that had been lost in a shipwreck, were stored in it.

Another story claims that Aoife fell in love with a man called Ilbhreac, the beloved of the sorceress Luchra, who cursed her rival and turned her into a crane (Monaghan, 2004).

Summary

The four examples of Celtic warrior women explored in this chapter highlight the diverse roles that women warriors played. First, we discussed Cartimandua, who is primarily remembered for her loyalty to the Romans. She could also be venerated as a peacemaker—as a queen who remained loyal to Rome to ensure that her kingdom stayed prosperous and stable. The alternative option of rebelling and destabilizing her domains would have threatened the lives and livelihoods of her subjects, indicating why her choice was one worthy of praise.

Two of the other women explored here are known for being the teachers of great warriors. Scáthach famously taught the hero Cú Chulainn martial arts and also initiated him as a warrior by becoming his lover. Her sister, Aífe, also played a role in the hero's initiation by fighting him and later submitting to him in defeat, allowing him to have sexual relations with her and bearing his son, Connla.

Similarly, Liath Luachra instructed a young Fionn mac Cumhaill in the art of war before the enemies that were hunting him forced her to leave him. Due to his young age and her "hideous" appearance, the hero and his guardian did not become lovers. However, they later reunited, resulting in the woman warrior's death, as she was either accidentally or deliberately killed by her nephew.

Notably, the three mythical examples are all perceived as fearsome women and excellent warriors. Although medieval scribes did their best to present Scáthach and Aífe as succumbing to the greater strength of Cú Chulainn, they deserve to be remembered as autonomous, successful, independent women who did not need a man in their lives. In this sense, they are great examples that independent women today can take inspiration from.

These last two chapters have made it apparent that there was a spiritual dimension to women leaders in the Celtic period. Boudica is recorded as having evoked the goddess Andraste and having acted as a high priestess of her cult, while Queen Medb is presented as an ageless, semi-divine figure. Aífe has been equated with Epona, the horse goddess, and she and Scáthach are believed to be semi-divine. These ideas will be explored further in the next chapter, where we look at the role of priestesses and their spiritual leadership in the Celtic world.

Chapter Four

Priestesses

Spiritual Leadership

I see a battle: a fair man
With much blood about his belt
And a hero, halo around his head,
His brow is full of victories.

– from "The Táin"

HERE, WE LOOK AT female spiritual leadership in Celtic society, considering the evidence for the existence of female Druidesses that can be found in legend and Classical source material, as well as the role of priestesses in the Celtic world. This section also considers historical and mythological examples of female spiritual leaders, such as Brigid, who began as a goddess and was transformed into a saint in the Middle Ages, and the priestesses Veleda and Ganna.

Female Spiritual Leadership in Celtic Society

According to Irish tradition, there were two main names for Druid women: *banduri* (or *bandorai*), and *banfilld*, denoting female poets (Klimczak, 2016). Accounts of Celtic female Druidesses, priestesses, and seers are found in both myth and historical sources. However, sometimes, it is difficult to separate historical figures from mythology, as these examples may have been based on real women while some Classical accounts may have been fabricated or, at least, heavily exaggerated.

In addition, across the Celtic world, there were connections between women, prophecy, and other magical powers. The Celts believed that women were uniquely gifted with divination. Tacitus noted that the Germanic tribes also believed that women were often blessed with this ability to predict the future. In addition to Tacitus, Julius Caesar and Strabo also talk of the presence of Germanic priestesses with prophetic capabilities who made predictions about the outcomes of war (Green, 1997).

The Druidess in Myth

The body of Celtic myth and legend abounds with accounts of Druids, poets, and magicians. Many of these practitioners were men, although Celtic tradition tells us of several legendary or divine women who also possessed these skills. The goddesses Macha, Brigid, and The Morrígan are all credited with the gift of prophecy, while the mythical warrior and martial arts teacher, Scáthach, made prophecies to the hero Cú Chulainn about his dynasty. In doing this, she used the power of *imbas forosnai* ("great knowledge of illumination"), which was one of the most important aspects of the Celtic spiritual wisdom tradition (MacLeod, 2014).

Several Druidesses are mentioned in myths. Early Irish legends say that Fionn mac Cumhaill was raised by two women, a Druidess and a wise woman who guarded, advised, and taught him the arts of war, hunting, and fishing. The latter of whom would be Liath Luachra, discussed in

Chapter 2. Also, a woman called Duiblind ("Dark Pool") was depicted as an honored and esteemed figure and is called a Druidess, poetess, and seer in the text (MacLeod, 2014).

While these mythological accounts suggest that female Druids existed in Celtic society, the historical evidence is less clear, as it is unclear whether such women were truly Druidesses or instead priestesses or seers.

Druidesses in Celtic Society

Historical sources tell us that there were both male and female Druids, as they appear to mention several women who lived in the ancient Celtic world who may have been considered Druidesses. For example, Diocletian is said to have consulted a woman described as a *dryadas* ("a woman Druid") from the Belgic Tungri. Using a similar term, and writing in the fourth and fifth centuries C.E., Lampridius mentions a woman he calls a *mulier dryadas* (MacLeod, 2014).

While these women are referred to by terms that appear to mean "female Druid," in surviving Classical anecdotes they only perform divination. This suggests that these women may have been seers rather than official Druidic figures. However, it is also possible that they were and that the Roman interest in them focused on their prophetic abilities (MacLeod, 2014).

What is indisputable is that women were heavily involved in divinatory spiritual practices in the Celtic world. An account by Julius Caesar tells us that in certain Germanic communities, women were responsible for using divination to decide whether a tribe should wage war. This practice may have also taken place in other parts of Celtic Europe. In legend, one story from the *Ulster Cycle* says that the Druids at the court of Queen Medb prevented her from engaging in battle when the omens were bad (Green, 1997).

However, surviving sources mention female Druids far less frequently than their male counterparts, perhaps because of the Roman Empire's patriarchal view of the world. Despite this, accounts of these figures survive, such as a description of the Battle of Moytura, which states that two Druidesses enchanted the rocks and the trees to support the Celtic army. Meanwhile, Strabo wrote of a group of religious women who lived on an island near the Loir River (Klimczak, 2016).

A fascinating but questionable series of references were made about Druidesses in a group of late Roman literary sources known as the *Scriptores Historae Augustiae,* more commonly known as the *Augustan Histories,* which consists of texts allegedly written in the fourth century C.E. by several authors (Green, 1997). This collection includes *Lives of the Later Caesars,* a series of accounts of the more recent Roman emperors, some of whom had encounters with Druidesses.

For example, Vopiscus of Syracuse in Sicily speaks of two late third-century emperors who had such encounters: Diocletian and Aurelian. The latter is said to have directly contacted the women to obtain information about his descendants; however, he did not hear what he wanted to:

> On a certain occasion, Aurelian consulted the Druid priestesses in Gaul and enquired of them whether the imperial power would remain with his descendants, but they replied ... that none would have a name more illustrious in the commonwealth than the descendants of Claudius.
>
> Green, 1997: 97

By way of contrast, Diocletian's encounter with a Druidess took place entirely through chance. Vopiscus's grandfather described the event that took place while the emperor was serving in the ranks of the Roman army.

The Druidess came up to him when he was paying the bill at a tavern and told him off for not giving a tip. He merrily replied that when he was emperor, he would be more generous with his money. The Druidess scolded him for his flippancy but correctly predicted that he would indeed become the Roman ruler once he had slain "the boar" (*aper* in Latin). This vague statement was a riddle, meaning that he had to kill the Prefect of the Praetorian Guard before he became emperor. That prefect's name was Aper (Green, 1997).

Another author who contributed to the *Augustan Histories* was Aelius Lampridius, who tells us about the prophecy of a Gaulish Druidess who saw the future of the third-century emperor, Severus Alexander: "Furthermore, as he went to war, a Druid prophetess cried out in the Gallic tongue: "Go, but do not hope for victory, and put no trust in your soldiers"(Green, 1997: 97). The ruler was then promptly murdered by some of his men.

Although these examples may not be true, they do seem to affirm that female Druids, prophetesses, seeresses, or other holy women were commonplace in Celtic society.

Some more solid evidence substantiating the existence of female Druids appears in Tacitus's works from the first century C.E. During Boudica's revolt, a large number of Roman troops were in the western region of Britain pursuing a group of Druids because they were a threat due to their social and political power (MacLeod, 2014). Despite official policy, the Romans were generally tolerant of native spiritual practices. However, it was also policy to break up any organized religious or aristocratic influence that might develop into resistance or rebellion (MacLeod, 2014).

Before the revolt, in 43 C.E., Emperor Claudius had banned Druidism across the Empire. In 60 or 61 C.E., at the time of Boudica's rebel activity, this edict gave the Romans the authority to sack or destroy the Druid holy stronghold on Mona, as it was called by the Romans. In modern Welsh, the location is known as Môn or Anglesey in English (Guiley, 2008).

The invaders caught up with the Druids on Mona, where they had been attempting to escape to the safety of Ireland. Here, the Roman troops encountered a closely packed force of armed men interspersed with women who were "dressed like Furies in funeral black, with streaming hair and brandishing torches" (MacLeod, 2014: 148). All around the women were the Druids, with their hands raised to the skies and offering curses against the attackers.

Tacitus says that it was the Banduri who defended the island (Klimczak, 2016). He tells of black-clad Druidesses leaping among the Celtic warriors, howling to the gods, and screaming curses at the Romans. The attacking troops were so astonished by what they saw that they stopped in their tracks and were unable to move. Their commanders had to urge them to remain composed and kill the enemy rather than be afraid of "a mass of fanatical women" (MacLeod, 2014: 148). Eventually, the Romans won the battle and killed the warriors and the Druids, laying to waste the sacred groves (Guiley, 2008).

It is unclear whether these women were Banduri or the wives of the Druids mentioned in the account by Tacitus (MacLeod, 2014). One possibility is also that the Classical sources failed to differentiate between Druidesses and priestesses.

The Celtic world had its virgin holy women in the form of priestesses. These were virgins who performed spiritual functions, such as seeing prophecies and making devotions to particular gods or goddesses. Significantly, some of the most powerful religious functionaries of the Classical world were the Vestal Virgins, whose role was to keep alight the sacred flame of the Roman goddess Vesta.

The need for them to be sexually pure may have arisen from the perception that this was desirable when contacting the divine world. Virgins were considered to be potent symbols of fertility and regeneration. Their sexual energy was intact and had not been squandered on mortals, so it could be preserved for the gods (Green, 1997).

The Roman writer Pomponius Mela, who lived in the first century C.E., wrote of the holy inhabitants of Sena, one of a group of islands called the Cassiterides which, from his descriptions of their geographical location, are the modern Isles of Scilly, off the southwest tip of England. He says that on Sena, there was a Gaulish oracle attended to by nine virgin priestesses who were able to predict the future, cure all illnesses, and control the elements. Significantly, the number of holy women is a multiple of three, a sacred number to the Celts (Green, 1997).

Fertility Cults

Fertility was a core concern for the Celts, as it perpetuated human and animal life and also meant that life could be sustained through crops and nature. Thus, the prosperity of all creatures and natural phenomena was important to the Celts. As such, divine powers associated with the fruitfulness of humans, livestock, and crops were objects of veneration.

Celtic spirits, such as the three-woman Matres were associated with the fertility of the land. These mothers were responsible for the earth's bounty, and they were depicted on altars with baskets of fruit on their laps and accompanied by acolytes bearing garlands of flowers (Green, 1997; Sullivan, 2024).

Cauldrons were a symbol of fertility for the Celts and were associated with inexhaustibility, inspiration, and regeneration, all properties relating to fecundity. The objects were associated with Dagda, the fertility god, and Ceridwen and Branwen, the goddesses of fertility and love, respectively (MacCulloch et al., 2023).

There is not much evidence relating to women's participation in fertility cults. However, accounts do survive of related Celtic rituals. Pliny the Elder recorded one brutal ritual that was practiced to guarantee the abundance of livestock and the prosperity of the community in his *Natural History*, which was written in the first century C.E.

In this work, he recalled a religious ceremony that was conducted by Druids in Gaul. He recalls how the religious leaders first cut down mistletoe that had been growing upon a sacred oak before sacrificing two white bulls. The cuttings were used as a cure for infertility. He also says that the Druids saw the plant as the most sacred of their kind. Pliny adds:

> Mistletoe is rare and when found, it is gathered with great ceremony, particularly on the sixth day of the moon ... Hailing the moon in a native word that means "healing all things," they prepare a ritual sacrifice and banquet beneath a tree and bring up two white bulls, whose horns are bound for the first time on this occasion. A priest arrayed in white vestments climbs the tree and with a golden sickle cuts down the mistletoe, which is caught in a white cloak. Then finally they kill the victims, praying to God to render his gift propitious to those on whom he has bestowed it. They believe that mistletoe given in drink will impart fertility to any barren animal and that it is an antidote to all poisons.
> Pliny, Natural History XVI, 95 cited in Green, 1997: 18

Pliny's account shows how the Celtic religion and practice were concerned with healing and fertility, and how mistletoe was used in both.

There is no mention of cults being led by priestesses despite the heavy association between fecundity and women in Celtic culture. The abundance of nature has long been associated with female deities, as the waxing and waning of the moon was associated with fertility due to its links to the length of the menstrual cycle (Morris, 1991). Nevertheless, women were heavily tied to and involved in religious activity related to this concern in the Celtic world.

Female Participation in Seasonal Festivals

Both men and women also actively participated in the Celtic seasonal festivals of Imbolc, Beltane, Lughnasadh, and Samhain because the movement of the seasons required equal amounts of masculine and feminine energy to retain natural balance (Tanishka, 2017).

The need for equilibrium is significant, as many Celtic festivals focused on the prosperity of the land, something related to feminine energy. Particularly, the May occasion of Beltane celebrating the beginning of summer included the Druidic fire ritual, in which cattle were driven between two bonfires in what served as a fertility and purification rite (Green, 1997).

The moon was another important aspect of the Celtic religion. Caesar and Pliny both report that the Druids recorded time by tracking the movements of the moon. Furthermore, Celtic goddesses associated with healing and regeneration are sometimes depicted wearing Luna amulets. The great temple to the healer goddess Sulis Minerva at Bath was also adorned with a carving of the Roman moon goddess, Luna (Green, 1997; Sullivan, 2024). Notably, the lunar symbol is associated with fertility. These examples indicate that the Celts believed that the moon played some role in the healing process and fecundity, both of which were key womanly concerns. It is worth noting that the association between feminine spirituality, divine femininity, and moon worship means that the moon continues to play a central role in modern pagan practices.

Brigid the Bright—From Pagan to Christian Saint

Brigid ("Exalted One") was a Celtic goddess who turned into a saint following Ireland's conversion to Christianity.

Brigid the Pagan Goddess

Brigid was a goddess of the Tuatha Dé Danann and a daughter of the chief of the gods, The Dagda (NicGrioghair, 2024). However, while Cormac mac Cuilennáin, a 10th-century Irish scholar, bishop, and king, described her as the god's daughter, other sources say she was his mother or wife (Condren, 1989). She was the goddess of fire, fertility, smithing, crops, cattle, and poetry.

She is the most powerful female religious figure in Irish history. At various points in time, she has been seen as a triple goddess, lawmaker, virgin mother, virgin saint, and folk hero (Condren, 1989). Although Brigid is primarily an Irish cultural figure, she is also associated with the roles and functions of goddesses of other cultures, such as the Roman Minerva or the Greek Aphrodite.

There is also a relationship between Brigid and the Divine Feminine, as she is depicted as having all the qualities possessed by the "good female," namely, being compassionate, nurturing, and loving (Condren, 1989; Berg, 2022). Early Irish sagas that include the goddess depict her as a beloved figure embodying many aspects of the concept. She is commonly presented as a healer, poetess, and smith-worker—roles that encompass nurturing care, creative inspiration, and transformative power.

Brigid's example reveals how deeply entwined spiritual vitality was with practical activities for early Celts; her realms were both hearthside and cosmic. The fact that she is associated with these healing, poetry, and smithing indicates that she was another tripartite goddess. Some say that she is three separate women, perhaps sisters (Weber, 2015; Sullivan, 2024).

Another way of seeing Brigid is as a force for transformation and vitality. This is because she embodies the qualities of both the young lady and the hag. As a young woman, she was known for her beauty. In her later years, she became a wise and sage-like figure. Significantly, the Triple Goddess, who Brigid is closely associated with, represents the iterations of womanhood: maiden, mother, and crone. As Brigid embodies all three, she is a powerful figure in Celtic spirituality (Berg, 2022; Sullivan, 2024).

Brigid was said to have the gift of prophecy and was worshipped by the *fili* (Britannica, 2024b), made up of poets and historians. According to Cormac mac Cuilennáin, writing in his *Glossary*:

> Brigid, that is the female poet, daughter of the Dagda. That is Brigit the female seer, or woman of insight, i.e., that goddess whom poets used to worship, for her cult was very great and very splendid. It is for this reason that they call her the goddess of poets by this title.
>
> Weber, 2015: 1

In honor of the goddess, the chief poet always carried a golden branch with tinkling bells (Condren, 1989). This gesture symbolizes her role as patroness of the poet class.

Brigid the Christian Saint

Following conversion to Christianity, the church transformed the goddess Brigid into a Christian saint around 453 C.E. Saint Brigid is the patroness of cattle and farm work and is said to protect the household from fire and calamity (NicGrioghair, 2024), so she retained the Celtic goddess of the same name's pastoral function. She was believed to be the daughter of Dubthach, a Druid who took her from Ireland to be raised on the Isle of Iona.

Her feast day is February 1, which was also the date the pagan festival of Imbolc took place (Britannica, 2024b). Notably, in February 2023, Saint Brigid's Day became a new national holiday in the country with the day's namesake being seen as a "representative of divinity who can empower female people" (Bero, 2023).

In the Hebrides, one belief associated with the saint is that she was the foster mother of Christ. In Gaelic, she is commonly called *Muime Chriosd* ("Foster-Mother of Christ"), demonstrating the intermingling of Christian and pagan influence. Interestingly, bestowing the status of foster mother on Brigid allows her to receive exceptional honor because, in Celtic society, foster parents had a special place, ranking higher than natural parents, with the relationship considered to be especially sacred (NicGrioghair, 2024).

Brigid's story merges the divine with the mortal, thereby overlapping and intersecting myth with reality. MacKillop (1998) tells how the story of the mythical Brigid has become intertwined with that of the saint of Kildare (d. 525), one of the three patron saints of Ireland. This Brigid is thought to have been born in the mid-fifth century at Faughart, near Dundalk, County Louth, and to have founded a religious house at Kildare, where she died. Interestingly, one of her symbols is the serpent, and her sanctuary may have been a cult center for the snake (Condren, 1989). As not much is known about this historical figure, it would have been easy to combine her story with that of the Celtic goddess.

Brigid's long afterlife means that her spiritual legacy and influence are still keenly felt today. Her connection to the Divine Feminine means that she has the potential to be a powerful role model for modern women. In a world that tends to value power and success over empathy and compassion, her example reminds us of the importance of feminine power, as she shows us that it is possible to be kind and loving while remaining strong and powerful. Her feminine qualities combined with her powerful nature make her the ideal figurehead for the modern feminist cause and women's rights advocacy.

Notable Seeresses and Prophetesses

Veleda

While Veleda is often considered to be a Celtic Druidess, this designation is controversial, as she originated from a Germanic tribe, not a Celtic-speaking region of Germany. Nevertheless, she is an interesting figure because the customs and practices of her people are similar to many Celtic ones, making her example relevant here.

Tacitus explained that the most powerful woman blessed with the power of divination in the Germánic tribes was Veleda, a virgin who enjoyed divine status and was her tribe's political negotiator. She was the seeress to the Bructeri, a Germanic people who came to prominence during the Batavian rebellion of 69–70 C.E., headed by the Romanized Batavian chieftain, Gaius Julius Civillis.

"Veleda" is not so much a name as it is a title. It comes from the Proto-Celtic welet, which translates to "seer" and is a derivative from the root "wel-," meaning "to see" (Delamarre, 2003). However, she did not come from a region where the Celtic languages were spoken, so perhaps the West-Germanic word waldon ("to have power") better conveys the meaning of her name or title (Lendering, 2006).

The ancient Germanic people believed that prophetesses like Veleda were living goddesses. Notably, the Bructeri maintained that many of their women had the gift of prophecy (MacLeod, 2014). Consequently, the seeress was regarded as a deity by most of the tribes in Central Germany and enjoyed wide influence over them (Peck, 1965). She lived in a tower near the Lippe, a river that connects to the Rhine, where she was often consulted by her tribesmen and other visitors.

On one occasion, the inhabitants of Colonia Claudia Ara Agrippinensium (modern-day Cologne) accepted her arbitration in a conflict with the

Tencteri, a German tribe outside the boundaries of the Roman Empire. However, the envoys were not allowed to be in her presence. Instead, an interpreter conveyed their messages to Veleda and reported her replies (Frazer, 1947). In his *Histories, IV 65* Tacitus explains that:

> But any approach to Veleda or speech with her was forbidden. This refusal to permit the envoys to see her was intended to enhance the aura of veneration that surrounded the prophetess. She remained immured in a high tower, one of her relatives being deputized to transmit questions and answers as if he were mediating between a god and his worshippers.
>
> Green, 1997: 97

The fact that the people of Cologne accepted her arbitration indicates that she had great authority across Germany.

Veleda's decision to live in isolation, communicating only through interpreters (most likely her relatives) suggests that she was a priestess rather than a Druidess. In some instances, Celtic priestesses appear to have lived apart from society in sacred communities, although some lived and worked among their people or served as priestesses for a particular deity (MacLeod, 2014).

Perhaps Veleda's most famous exercise of her talents was that she successfully predicted the original success of the rebels against the Roman legion during the Batavian rebellion. She may have prophesized the rebellion, or her pronouncements may have been what started it (Lendering, 2006). Her remote position as a goddess in a tower may have made her divination of these events unclear.

In this conflict, Batavian forces were first raised by their leader, Civilis, in 69 C.E. in allegiance with Vespasian during the Roman power struggle.

However, once the rebel leader became aware of the weakened condition of the legions in Romanized Germany, he openly revolted. The conflict intensified in 70 C.E. when the Batavians were joined by Julius Classicus and Julius Tutor, leaders of the Treviri, who were also Roman citizens. The rebellion enjoyed some initial successes when the Roman garrison at Novaesium, or modern-day Neuss, surrendered without a fight, as did another at Castra Vetera, which was near modern-day Xanten in Niederrhein, Germany (Grant, 1974).

The commander of the first garrison to submit, Munius Luperus was sent to Veleda; however, he was killed in an ambush en route. On another occasion, the Praetorian trireme (flagship) was captured and rowed upriver on the Lippe, along with its loot, as a gift to Veleda (Lendering, 2006; Parker, 2016). These offerings are indicative of her high status and her leadership role in her tribe.

The rebellion collapsed following a strong show of force by nine Roman legions under Gaius Licinius Mucianus. Civilis was cornered on his home island of Batavia by a force headed by Quintus Petillius Cerialis. The Batavian leader's fate is unknown. What is known is that Cerialis treated the rebels leniently to reconcile them to Roman rule and military service (Grant, 1974). This meant Veleda enjoyed several more years of liberty and status as a powerful priestess.

Her position was eventually usurped a few years after the rebellion. Between 75 and 78 C.E., Rutilius Gallicus, governor of Lower Germany, launched a series of successful campaigns against the Bructeri. In 77 C.E., the Romans eventually either captured Veleda and took her as a hostage or gave her asylum. The Latin poet Statius tells us that she was taken captive by Rutilius (Henderson, 1998). In a poem written in 89 C.E. celebrating the governor's career, he recalls:

> Time lacks to set forth the armies of the north and rebel Rhine, the prayers of the captive Veleda, and, greatest and

> latest glory, Rome placed in your charge as the Dacians
> were perishing, where you, Gallicus, were chosen to take
> the reins from so great a ruler to Fortune no surprise.
>
> Parker, 2016: 285

After her capture, Veleda may have acted in Roman interests, negotiating the acceptance of a pro-Roman king by the Bruteri in 83 or 84 C.E. (Lendering, 2006). Further information about her life from this point came to light with the discovery of a fragmentary Greek inscription published in 1947. The text appears to have been part of a satire, in which someone, perhaps Vespasian, asks the oracle: "What should be done concerning the tall maiden … whom the Rhine dwellers worship, shuddering at the thunderings of her golden voice" (Parker, 2016: 285).

From the context of this inscription, the seeress appears to have become a temple servant at Ardea, near Rome. This suggests that Veleda's religious role as a priestess among the Bructeri continued to inform her position and status in Italy. Her example shows how foreign leaders formerly at war with Rome could be incorporated into the Empire following their submission.

Ganna: Druidess Diplomat

Just one Classical source survives that tells us about Ganna. In his *Roman History*, Cassius Dio makes a brief reference to Emperor Domitian, the son of Vespasian who ruled from 81 to 96 C.E., having an audience with Veleda's successor, a virgin priestess from Germany called Ganna. She had gone on an official trip to Rome accompanied by Masyos, king of the Semnones tribe (Klimczak, 2016; Telyndru, 2023).

Dio tells us: "Masyos, king of the Semnones, and the virgin Ganna, who had appeared as a seeress in Celtica after Veleda, came to Domitian, were treated honorably and were returned" (Simek, 2020: 279). The visit to Rome probably took place in 86 C.E., a year after Masyos's final war with the Chatti and after he made a treaty with the Cherusci, who lived between the rivers Elbe and the Weser (Simek, 2020).

Like Veleda before her, Ganna likely served a diplomatic role in negotiations with the emperor. The role of seeress appears to have existed as an office among the Germanic tribes, and it seems that Veleda was succeded by Ganna in this position (Enright, 1996).

Some clues about who she was and the role she served in the Semnones tribe can perhaps be inferred from her name. The name "Ganna" may come from the Old Norse word *gandr* meaning "magic wand." Alternatively, it may relate to the Proto-Celtic word *geneta* for "girl" (Telyndru, 2023). As she was a virgin priestess or Druidess, both words have some relation to who she was and her role in the society in which she lived.

Surviving manuscripts tell us that Ganna lived in Celtica, but the campaign she is associated with took place in Germanica, east of the Rhine, and was led by Emperor Domitian in the eighth decade of the first century C.E. (Simek, 2020). It would have been her job as a seeress to be present during dealings between the Romans and the Germanic tribes. Ganna's influence is demonstrated by how she was taken to Rome with Masyos, the king of her tribe, and how both were treated with honors before returning home. This suggests that her right was equal to that of her chief (Simek, 2020).

Ganna is sometimes said to be a Druidess; however, the limited sources available do not make it clear whether this was the case or not (Telyndru, 2023). Instead, they simply describe her as a virgin prophetess. This seems to suggest that she had a spiritual function within her tribe. For example, Simek (2020) proposes that she taught the art of prophesying to a younger tribeswoman named Waluburg, who went on to serve as a seeress at the First Cataract of the Nile in Egypt.

The examples of Ganna and her predecessor, Veleda, indicate that spiritual leadership was commonly bestowed on Celtic women and that these women taught one another these crafts so that the traditions survived from generation to generation.

Summary

Here, we have seen that women played key religious leadership roles in Celtic society. One of Ireland's most powerful deities, both before and after the advent of Christianity is Brigid, first as the goddess Brigid and since as Saint Brigid. The Celts also venerated women such as Veleda and Ganna, who they believed had the power to see the future. Womanly concerns, such as fertility and healing, were also key concerns of the Celtic religion. In the next chapter, we continue our exploration in a similar vein, considering the position of wise women such as seers, healers, and poets in Celtic society.

Chapter Five
Wise Women

Healers, Seers, Poets

I met a lady in the meads,
Full beautiful—a faery's child,
Her hair was long, her foot was light,
And her eyes were wild [...]
I set her on my pacing steed,
And nothing else saw all day long,
For sidelong would she bend, and sing
A faery's song.

– John Keats,
from "La Belle Dame sans Merci"

IN THIS CHAPTER, WE explore another type of powerful woman in Celtic society: the wise woman. She could be a healer, seer, or poet. Unlike female rulers, warriors, and even some seers, she did not have a political function. This demonstrates that the Celts appreciated that not all powerful women in this world have to fulfill a traditionally "male" role. What a wise woman was and how that role was connected to the afterlife is explored below, along with some examples of such women in Celtic myth.

The Celtic Wise Woman

Examples of "wise" people have been found across the Celtic world well into recent times (Curran, 2010). These figures were a part of all Celtic communities and tribes and, whether they were men or women, acted as local doctors, detectives, and divinators. They were often said to have acquired the magical powers they possessed through supernatural means.

Druids are one example of those who enjoyed this position in Celtic societies, and Julius Caesar speaks of them as having both religious and secular influence. Additionally, seeresses or prophetesses were also commonplace. They were believed to have the power to look into the future and predict the outcome of war and conflict, so the wise woman could also predict either prosperity or doom (Morris, 1991; Green, 1997).

Despite the prominent position of Druids in Celtic society, powers of prophecy and healing are more often associated with women in this world. This could be because of the links between women and the moon, the latter of which was believed to control the menstrual cycle and was also a symbol of death. Consequently, priestesses and other Celtic wise women had a dualistic nature because of their association with both life, through fertility and healing, as well as death. This was symbolized by the witch figure.

The figure of the Celtic wise woman survives in the form of strong local traditions and folk stories. But what evidence exists for the role they played in the Celtic period? As it turns out, there is quite a lot.

The Celts themselves left accounts of women performing magic. One such example is the inscription discovered in a tomb in Larzac, southern France in 1983. An inscribed lead sheet was found there on a tablet broken into two pieces, which had covered a pot containing the remains of a woman. On the sheet's four sides were 160 words in Gaulish, written using a Latin script. This amounts to an account of the presence of two rival groups of female magicians ("women endowed with magic") and the text describes how one group had attempted to harm the other through magical means. The wronged set of magicians had then employed wise women to neutralize the evil charm (Green, 1997; Sullivan, 2024).

This example shows that magical practices among Celtic women were organized and regulated into guilds and covens, indicating that these powers were seen as real and respected as a force in their own right in Celtic society.

Archaeological remains also attest to the existence of women with these abilities in the Celtic world. Excavators of the Romano-British cemetery at Lankhills, Winchester found that it contained burials of several old women dating to the fourth century C.E. They had been decapitated, and their heads had been placed by their legs.

A similar pattern of ritual behavior has been found in other Celtic cemeteries studied in Britain. A very specific rite took place at Kimmeridge in Dorset in the late third century C.E. In this cemetery, the bodies of elderly women had been decapitated and laid to rest with their lower jaws removed and their heads positioned by their feet. Each body was also accompanied by a spindle whorl (Green, 1997; Sullivan, 2024).

This arrangement of remains was common in Celtic times, as this was a way of positioning the dead in the direction of the Otherworld. However, the removal of the lower jaw implies a desire to prevent the deceased person from speaking. It may have been that these women were known to have cast spells in life and that the community was worried that they might continue to do this in death unless they were explicitly prevented from doing so (Green, 1997).

The presence of spindle whorls in the graves of the Kimmeridge women is also significant, as in the Classical and Celtic religions, this is a symbol of fate and destiny. The Roman Fates and some Gaulish Mother Goddesses were perceived to be able to predict the life and death of humans, and they could also end lives by snapping the thread of their spindles. The presence of the objects in the graves may therefore suggest that whoever buried them believed that they also possessed this ability (Green, 1997).

The figure of the wise woman survived the Celtic period and several examples of others engaging in similar practices to those of their ancestors have been recorded in Ireland and Cornwall. In the 19th century, Biddy Earle of County Clare and Moll Anthony of County Kildare both had their powers denounced by the church.

Biddy was supposed to have acquired her powers supernaturally through a blue bottle given to her by the ghost of one of her former husbands. Meanwhile, Moll possessed a glass that allowed her to glimpse the future, much as Celtic seers and prophetesses had done. She had been given her glass by the fairies of the Hill of Grange where she lived, and she was said to be on the friendliest of terms with them. She was also able to cure animals (and sometimes humans) simply by touching them (Curran, 2010).

Wise people also flourished in Cornwall and were known as "pellars," a shortened form of "repeller." The name is related to the belief that they were able to drive away disease, misfortune, and curses.

One of the most famous Cornish wise women was Tamsin Blight (Tammy Blee), also known as "the Witch of Helson," who lived between 1798 and 1856. She had been single and lived alone for most of her life, marrying only at the age of 38. She plied her trade as a pellar, issuing charms, performing conjuring, and claiming to be of "true pellar blood" stretching back to Celtic antiquity (Curran, 2010: 157).

She was best known as a seller of much sought-after talismans and charms, which were designed to lift curses or ward away evil luck. Many of the amulets were mere pieces of paper with supposedly mystical words written on them. For an extra fee, the pellar would add a bizarre design to increase the potency of her charm. Some examples include "a headless cherub" and "a brooding angel or bird" drawn on one side of the paper (Curran, 2010: 158). On others, she wrote quasi-Biblical names like "Jehovah," "Jah," "Elohim," or "Adonay." She also sold rings or pendants that were supposed to bring luck and fend off evil spirits (Curran, 2010).

These examples of 19th-century wise women show how ancient Celtic practices survived and demonstrate the kinds of activities their Celtic counterparts may have indulged in.

Traditional Healing Practices by Wise Women

The Celts engaged in a wide variety of traditional healing practices, including curative rituals, herbalism, and water therapy.

Various healing rituals were performed in the Celtic period at stone cromlechs and dolmens, often set high on hillsides. According to an account by Julius Caesar:

> The whole nation of the Gauls is greatly devoted to ritual observances, and for that reason those who are smitten with the more grievous maladies and who are engaged in the perils of battle either sacrifice human victims or vow to do so, employing the Druids as ministers for such sacrifices. They believe, in effect, that unless for a man's life, a man's life may be paid, the majesty of the immortal gods may not be appeased.
>
> Shephard, 2015: 249

The sacred practices of the Druids were thought to bring about healing and rejuvenation. Plants were used both for medicinal purposes and in religious rituals. For example, in his *Natural History XXIV,* Pliny notes that the Druids of Gaul recommended the *Selago* plant for diseases of the eyes and as something that could be kept on the person to ward off fatalities (Green, 1997).

The Celts also associated healing with magic. In the same book, Pliny observes that they believed that the *Selago* had to be collected in a specific way to be effective. That was, "without iron with the right hand, thrust under the tunic through the left arm-hole as though the gatherer were thieving" (Green, 1997: 46).

Other plants, such as mistletoe, were also used for both medicinal and magical purposes. The plant was used in rituals and also given to sick people as a drink. At the time, it was thought to be an effective infertility treatment and an antidote to all poisons (Green, 1997).

In the Celtic period, medicine was the domain of Druids, witches, shamans, and wise women. Celtic wise women acknowledged the links that existed between human life and creation as a whole. Thus, they focused their skills on assisting with matters of childbirth and making and distributing appropriate herbal remedies. They, along with, wizards also recognized the sacred properties that existed in 20 different types of trees, as demonstrated by the 20-letter ogham tree alphabet. The first letter of which was *Beithe*, representing the birch tree that signified youth, renewal, and rebirth. Meanwhile, the letter *Ngetal*, or reed, symbolized health, harmony, and growth (Shephard, 2015).

There was also an association between wise women and healing bodies of water in the Celtic period. Notably, they were the priestesses of wells. Saint Patrick found Irish pagans worshipping a well they called *Slan* ("health-giving"), performing rituals there and offering sacrifices to it (MacCulloch, 2023).

Additionally, it was during the Romano-Celtic period that the cult of Sulis Minerva which was based around the hot springs of Bath, England was established. In the sixth and seventh decades of the first century C.E., a magnificent complex was built in the town, funded by Rome, with construction organized by the Imperial army based there (Irby-Massie, 1999). The name "Sulis" itself relates to the Suleviae, a Celtic triad that was worshipped in Germany as goddesses of water, prosperity, fertility, and healing (Irby-Massie, 1999).

The example of the cult is likely reflective of religious activity around hot springs before the Roman invasion. Another form of evidence is the Celtic coins dating to the early first century C.E. that have been found in the King's Bath Spring. This shows how the Celts were well aware of the healing properties of water decades before the Roman invasion.

There is not much evidence concerning the activities of Celtic wise women during that period; however, the *bean feasa* (the "woman of knowledge") or the *bean leighis* (the "woman of healing") was a key figure in Celtic folk traditions. In Ireland and Scotland, there has always been a thriving tradition of powerful local female healers who often practiced herbalism and shared these practices with male healers.

Crucially, the wise woman was implicated in the wider health of the community as well as that of individuals. She was consulted by people to report "breaches of communitarian or cosmological harmony" (Blackie, 2019). This suggests that such a person was involved in both healing the individual medically from illness and the community socially if there was conflict within it.

It is also notable that wise women were viewed with a mixture of reverence and fear in Britain as late as the 16th century. For example, in his 1597 work *Daemonologie*, King James VI of Scotland and I of England warned against "The fearfull aboundinge ... in this countrie, of those detestable slaves of the Devill, the witch or enchanters" (Shephard, 2015: 250). On the other hand, in 1584, Reginald Scot strove to dispel the fear of wise women in his book *The Discoverie of Witchcraft*. These examples indicate that wise women prospered in Britain long after the Celtic period ended.

Seers and Poets

There is a strong link between seers and poets in the Celtic tradition. For example, the word fili, used to describe a high class of poets in Ireland has come to mean "poet," but in origin, its meaning is closer to "seer." At one time, the fili may have had some of the attributes of the Druids (Ross, 1970). Notably, they both entertained and had the power of divination. One example is the one who interpreted the dream of King Dermot of Tara (Condren, 1989).

The fili could practice divination by using various rites and have been accredited with the supernatural power of blemishing, or causing death, by satire. For example, in "The Táin," Queen Medb gets Ferdiad to fight in single combat against his friend and foster brother, Cú Chulainn by such means:

> Then Medb sent the Druids and satirists and harsh bards for Ferdiad, that they might make against him three satires to stay him and three lampoons, and that they might raise on his face three blisters, shame, blemish, and disgrace so that he might die before the end of nine days, if he did not succumb at once.
>
> Ross, 1970: 165

This example shows that poets had spiritual powers and could kill with their words. So, in a pagan society, these figures had a religious as well as a spiritual function.

There is plenty of evidence in myth and classical sources to support the idea that female seers were commonplace in the Celtic world. See Chapter 3 as well as the example of Fedelm, the prophetess who appears in "The Táin," later on in the chapter.

Fewer accounts of female poets survive. However, one appears in a ninth-century love poem. It tells of how Cuirithir, who was fiercely in love with Líadain, asked her to marry him, but she was in the middle of her professional bardic circuit around Ireland. She told him to wait until she had returned. However, he was anxious for them to have a son "who would be famous" (Condren, 1989: 97).

The poetess, realizing that motherhood would mean the end of her career, decided to take a vow of chastity. Cuirithir was distraught when he heard what she had done and followed suit with the same vow. Both of them then put themselves under the direction of the severe Saint Cummine. Initially, the pair were only allowed to talk to each other behind gravestones. Later, they were permitted to share a bed accompanied by a "little scholar." However, one night, the poets broke their vow. Afterward, Cuirithir was banished from the community and Líadain died of a broken heart (Condren, 1989).

The moral of this story is that sexuality is an obstacle to the divine. However, it also serves as an example of a woman choosing to prioritize her career over motherhood and demonstrates how much the skills of poets were valued in Celtic society. Although the tale suggests that Líadain was wrong to place her vocation over the chance of having a child, her position as a career woman resonates with us today.

While stories of Celtic poetesses are few and far between, Celtic mythology is full of stories of goddesses as sources of poetic inspiration, and such traditions are widespread. Two examples are Brigid, the Irish goddess and patroness of poets, and Ceridwen, the Welsh goddess of inspiration (Ross, 1970; Matthews, 2002).

In Irish mythology, the Otherworldly well of wisdom, called the Well of Segais or Conla's Well, is the ultimate source of knowledge. It is also the source of the River Boyne, named after the goddess Boann. According to the *Dindsenchas*, a collection of Celtic Irish myths, she went to test the well's power, challenging it by walking three times widdershins about it.

Three waves from the well then rose and drowned her (Matthews, 2002). Thus, she became the source of wisdom within the river.

Another story that links water to wisdom or inspiration is "The Adventures of Cormac" in the Land of Promise, an island of paradise. When King Cormac travels to the Otherworldly palace of Manannán mac Lir, the warrior king of the Otherworld and Irish sea god, he discovers a shining fountain. The deity explains his vision in the following way:

> The fountain which thou sawest, with the five streams are the five sources through which knowledge is obtained. And no one will have knowledge who drinks not a drought out of the fountain itself and out of the streams. The folk of many arts are those who drink them both.
>
> Matthews, 2002: 79

Therefore, bodies of water that were patronized by goddesses and Otherworldly figures were commonly seen as a source of artistic or poetic inspiration in the Celtic world.

Beliefs in the Death and Afterlife

The Celts believed in an afterlife. Archaeological investigations have shown that the graves of their leaders and members of the elite were filled with personal possessions, such as board games, armor, food, weapons, and precious objects (History Brought Alive, 2022). The practice of burying the dead with these accompaniments suggests that the Celts believed that the deceased would use them on their next journey and when they were in the afterlife.

The journey the dead embarked on was to the Otherworld, otherwise known as "the Land of the Living," the "Delightful Plain," the "Land of the Young," and *Tír na nÓg* in Irish. This place was located either underground or was an island in the sea. It was a mixture of several different lands, which meant that the Celts had no one word to describe where people went when they died (Heinz, 2010). The realm the dead passed on to was seen as being similar to the mortal world but without any of its negative aspects, like pain or sorrow. The Celts expected their departed to find no sickness, death, or old age there, and anticipated happiness lasting forever, with a day going on for 100 years (Britannica, 2023).

Unlike the idea of Heaven and Hell in Christianity, in the Celtic belief system, the behavior of the person in life would not affect where they ended up once they died. Instead, due to the existence of several different Otherworld realms, the individual could encounter or travel to various Otherworlds by chance or even return to normal life afterward (Heinz, 2010). This idea suggests that the Celts did not see death as final and separate from life as we do today.

Impact on Female Wisdom

The Celts were so accepting of wise women because their mythological system told them that women primarily performed the role of mediator between the physical realm and the Otherworld.

Notably, female figures were strongly associated with the journey and access to the Otherworld. Deer, both male and female, were believed to lead people there, and the Celts associated the animal with travel. It was often thought to shapeshift into beautiful women who would lead individuals on their journey from one world to another (Pratt, 2007).

Celtic myth depicts feminine beings as offering heroes access to the Otherworld. An example is the Irish Celtic voyage or vision stories. In these tales, a beautiful girl approaches the hero and sings to him. In it, she tells him of a happy land (the Otherworld), and, fascinated by what she sings about, the hero follows her, sailing away with her in a boat of glass. In one version of the story, the pair are never seen again. In another, the hero returns after what he thinks is a short amount of time, only to realize that all of his companions are dead and that he has been away in another realm for hundreds of years (Britannica, 2023).

This story demonstrates how the pleasures of love and sexuality were thought to be widely available in the Otherworld. Both men and women who traveled this land were often said to find lovers there who were physically perfect, skilled, excellent conversationalists, and all-around interesting people. So strong is its reputation for love that it is sometimes called *Tír na mBan* ("Land of Women"). The term "Land of Men" is not attributed to the Otherworld, but examples can be found, such as the Cornish tale "Cherry of Zennor," that show that the sexual companion to be found there was a pleasure available to women as well as (Rua, 2008).

As wise women often mediated people's relationship with the afterlife, their role often included elements of both spiritual guides and modern therapeutic psychologists. These women gained their power and authority because of how closely associated they were with the Otherworld and the knowledge, wisdom, and skill that the connection conferred (Blackie, 2019).

Examples From Celtic Myth

Macha the Prophetess

The prophetess Macha is often confused with the more famous Macha Mong Ruad, who was one of the claimants of the Kingdom of Ulster. Another woman by the name, which made up the tripartite deity, is Macha Sanraith, who came to live with the widower Crunniuc and brought him prosperity by marrying him, increasing his wealth, and bearing him children.

It has been suggested that Macha, the prophetess figure, could be part of a triple goddess, an otherworldly woman with three identities and multiple associations. She may have been seen as a trifunctional or a tripartite goddess, serving the three European functions of the priest (prophetess), warrior, and fertility figure (Mallory & Adams, 1997). She may also have been a goddess of the land, and her high status indicates she could have been a sovereignty goddess (MacKillop, 1998).

Macha the prophetess was the wife of Nemed mac Agnomain, a Druidic entity connected with the word for "shrine" (Puhvel, 1970). She was one of the first settlers in Ireland and played a significant role in "The Táin" (Mallory & Adams, 1997). It is said that it was in her honor that the first plains of Ireland were cleared of thick forests. After looking into the future and seeing the bloodshed that would afflict the country during the great cattle raid of Cooley, she died of heartbreak (Monaghan, 2014).

The third woman by this name, Macha Sanraith, also exhibited powers of prophecy. One day, she appeared to a wealthy, widowed farmer, Crunniuc mac Agnomain, and began keeping house for him. Before the first nightfall, she made a sunwise ritual right-hand turn, ensuring good fortune, before entering his bed. Soon, Crunniuc grew more prosperous because of their union, and she became pregnant by him (MacKillop, 1998).

At one point, the farmer announced that he would go to the great assembly of the Ulstermen—some say that this event was a great feast hosted by King Conchobar mac Nessa. Macha warned him not to speak of her there, but, as he watched Conchobar's chariots racing, Crunniuc immediately boasted that his wife could outrun them all. Stung by these words, Conchobar had Crunniuc seized and demanded that he prove his claim. Macha protested that she was pregnant but agreed to do so to defend her husband and spare his life (MacKillop, 1998).

According to legend, she managed to outpace the horses and win the race, despite being with child. However, the exertion took its toll, and she went into labor at the end of the race, giving birth to twins. Although she had saved her husband's life, her exertion led to her death. Before she died, she found the strength to issue a terrible blessing and a curse to the men of Ulster, symbolized by the twins she left behind. In her last words, the woman blessed the men of the land with great strength and power. But she also said that in the time of their greatest need, when danger threatened the very survival of the province, they would find that their powers had faded and that they were as weak and vulnerable as a woman giving birth (Visit Armagh, 2024).

Many years later, when Conchobar was still king, the curse struck, and the story of Ulster's struggle is told in "The Táin." At that point, Cú Chulainn emerged to defend the land and become one of Ireland's most famous heroes (Visit Armagh, 2024).

Fedelm: Prophetess Poet

Fedelm, or Fedelma, was a woman in the court of Queen Medb of Connacht (Klimczak, 2016). She is described as "the woman from the Fairy," referring to the Otherworld (Green, 1997: 102). She appears in "The Táin" and is the prophetess of Cruachain. She was said to have the power of *imbas forosnai*, which allowed her to tell Medb that the war in Ulster would end in defeat. When she was asked to predict the fortunes of the Connacht forces, she responded with a long, chilling poetic prophecy of doom, in which she said of Medb's army: "I see it crimson, I see it red" (Green, 1997: 102).

The prophetess is believed to have studied poetry and prophecy in Britain, with some myths saying she studied in Alba, the supernatural land belonging to Scáthach, and held a gold weaving rod in her hand, which was symbolic of oracular powers (MacLeod, 2014; Green, 1997). In "The Táin," she is described as an armed but beautiful young woman riding a chariot. In appearance, her blonde hair falls below her knees, she wears gold-clasped sandals, and she has three irises in each eye (MacKillop, 1998). This unique feature reflects her ability to see into all three cosmic realms (MacLeod, 2014). Patricia Lysaght (1986) suggests that the prophetess is a predecessor to the banshee of later folk tradition, hinting that the behavior and supernatural powers of the Celtic Druidesses were somewhat fearsome and terrifying to the beholder.

It has been proposed that the Fedelm that appears in "The Táin" is the same character as Fedelm Foltchain ("of the lovely hair"), who appears in a short Irish text called "Fedelm and Cú Chulainn" or *Ces Ulad*, which translates to "The Affliction of the Ulsterman" (Koch, 2006). The text is preserved in one imperfect 16th-century manuscript and has been interpreted very differently in two separate translations by John Carey and Vernam Hull (Bernhardt-House, 2009). However, we should apply some caution here as "Fedelm" is the name of many female personages, real and imaginary, in early Ireland and includes prophetesses, queens, and saints (MacKillop, 1998). Thus, the woman of the story could be a different person entirely.

What is intriguing though is that the Fedelm depicted in the tale also has the gift of imbas. According to the surviving fragments of the text, as translated by Carey, one day before the invasion, Cú Chulainn and his charioteer Laeg travel to the River Boyne to learn the skill. However, Hull translates this as "riches." Bernhardt-House (2009) suggests that the former is more likely in an early Irish narrative, as the banks of rivers were seen as having a connection to the Otherworld and would be a suitable place to obtain poetic wisdom.

Fedelm and her husband, Elcmaire stand on the opposite side of the bank. They notice Cú Chulainn, his charioteer, their board games, and birds. Elcmaire becomes upset when the warrior hero manages to catch a speckled salmon with his spear. In response, the older man goes into the ford and flings a pillar stone toward the chariot. In retaliation, Cú Chulainn cuts off both of the man's thumbs and both of his big toes.

After this, Fedelm utters either a prophecy (Carey) or a promise (Hull) that she will appear naked to the Ulstermen and become Cú Chulainn's lover. She does this after a year and a day. At the end of the text, it is suggested that the Ulstermen's debility was caused by the prophetess appearing to them (Koch & Carey, 2000). This story does not make much sense, but it does suggest that Fedelm's status as a wise woman was known outside of "The Táin."

Another story also hints at a connection between Fedelm and the River Boyne. In the second, a Middle Irish revised version of "Tochmarc Emire," when Cú Chulainn travels southward to woo Emer, he visits the *Smir*, or "Marrow of the woman Fedelm," this being another name for the River Boyne (O'Rahilly, 1975).

Learning From Wise Women

In Celtic times, wise women played a prominent role in society, healing the sick, offering wisdom, and seeing insight into the future. While the Roman Conquest and the advent of Christianity put an end to Celtic culture and its belief system, wise women were commonplace across Europe, particularly in Britain and Ireland up until the 19th century.

However, it seems like this figure no longer officially exists or is not recognized as such today. But this does not mean we cannot learn from these women, or that they are not still here, albeit in different guises. Think of a woman you look up to. Why do you look up to her? Most likely, it is due to her wisdom and insight—thus, wise women walk among us.

Below, are some key characteristics of wise women:

- A wise woman is knowledgeable, and she combines that with compassion, giving her wisdom. In a society that values learnedness, her combination of insight and caring gives her something that's lacking in others.

- Because she has lots of life experience, she has developed good judgment (or street smarts).

- Wise women understand how life is connected, such as how we relate to nature and other beings; she sees existence more deeply.

Essentially, the wise woman is a heroine who has returned from her journey, realizing that she belongs to herself and the land where she lives. She is ready to offer her knowledge and gifts in service to her community (Blackie, 2019). This understanding tells us that any of us can aspire to be a wise woman.

You, too, can be one of them if you have experienced life and all the adventures it entails. In *Women Who Run With the Wolves*, in the chapter "Battle Scars: Membership of the Scar Clan," Clarissa Pinkola Estes puts forward the theory that women's insight is rightfully earned by surviving all that life throws at her: "all the name-calling a woman has endured in her life, all the insults, all the slurs, all the traumas, all the wounds, all the scars" (2008: 386). So, based on your experience and acquired wisdom through adversity, you now have the qualifications to assist others in need.

Summary

In this chapter, we have delved deeper into the figure of the Celtic wise woman and her role in society. We found that such individuals were associated with healing and spirituality, particularly travel between the mortal realm and the Otherworld. We also looked at Celtic examples in myth, such as Macha and Fedelm. All these themes can inform us as to how wise women can help and inform us in the modern era, as she is an example of female empowerment that we can strive to achieve. In the next chapter, we will expand on this theme further by looking at powerful female figures in Celtic mythology.

Chapter Six
Powerful Female Figures in Celtic Mythology

I dropped the berry in a stream
And caught a little silver trout [...]
It had become a glimmering girl
With apple blossom in her hair
Who called me by my name and ran
And faded through the brightening air.

- W.B. Yeats,
from "The Song of Wandering Aengus

THE BOUNDARIES BETWEEN HISTORICAL and mythical figures from the Celtic period are often blurred. Because the Celts did not leave any written accounts of their history and culture, we are left to rely on Roman retellings of events, which often portray the Celts, their motives, and their actions in a negative way. As we've already discussed, this is especially true in the case of female leaders, as the Romans did not believe it proper for women to assume these roles. To them, it was a transgression of the "natural" order of things. Later on, key Celtic figures, such as the goddess Brigid or Saint Brigid, were absorbed into the Christian church, and their stories were given an entirely different meaning.

Women, Goddesses, Myth, and Celtic Society

The Celtic social structure allowed women to hold a high social position. We know that the Celts of the first millennium B.C.E. gave women ownership and personal agency. In addition, under Irish and Welsh law of this time, women could own property and had rights as the mistress of a household and as a mother in marriage (McCoppin, 2022). Furthermore, Celtic women are recorded as serving as governmental and marital leaders and soldiers in both mythic and historical records. For example, Plutarch tells us that Celtic women "acted as ambassadors in battles ... and sat on peace councils," and priestesses known as *banfathi* "accompanied troops into battle and were relied upon for advice and strategy" (McCoppin, 2022: 24).

Archaeological evidence also proves that female warriors were commonplace in Celtic society. For example, one Iron Age coin that was minted in the first century B.C.E. by the polity of Redones, a Breton tribe whose main urban center was at Rennes, shows a naked woman sitting astride a galloping horse. There is what looks like a shield in her right hand and a sword in her left.

Another find to support this is a bronze figure of a female warrior that was discovered in Brittany and dated to the first century B.C.E. She is wearing a goose-crested helmet, which is significant because the Celts associated the goose with aggression (McCoppin, 2022).

The fairly high social standing of Celtic women was directly related to the lasting power associated with the goddesses of their religion. One of the strongest indications of this is the sacred marriage practices between kings and priestesses, as the ritual awarded these women high religious authority (McCoppin, 2022).

Many of the powerful women encountered in Celtic lore may well have had real-life counterparts. It seems likely that several women who are lost to history, including their real names and historical events, found a place in the canon of Celtic mythology (especially Irish, Welsh, and Scottish legends) instead.

Take the example of the goddess Scáthach. Roman historian Ammianus Marcellinus talked of Celtic female warriors who were feared by the Romans. McCoppin (2022) observes that the individuals referred to by Marcellinus came from a long Celtic tradition that allowed women to train at "war colleges," like those portrayed in "The Táin," where Scáthach is described as training the warrior Cú Chulainn. This example shows how her position as a female warrior and instructor is likely based on her real-life counterparts.

In the Celtic belief system, the goddesses were associated with the natural world, which was central to the culture's life and its social system, as everyone relied on nature and agriculture to survive. As such, the Celts were grateful to the environment around them for life itself.

McCoppin (2022) proposes that the high positioning of goddesses in Celtic mythology may come from cultures that pre-date the Indo-European Celtic groups, but this is equally likely to have come from the Celts themselves, as women were viewed as being of equivalent status to men in their society.

However, Celtic culture became increasingly patriarchal following the Roman Conquest. Even with the prominence of goddesses, they are portrayed in conflicting ways. For example, sisters Scáthach and Aífe are depicted as independent warrior women, but each is nevertheless compelled to submit sexually to the teenage hero Cú Chulainn. This suggests that, while the sisters were depicted as not in need of men, medieval writers could not allow them to have control over their sexuality.

The conflicting portrayals of divine female beings may suggest differences between the beliefs of the Celts and of those who recorded their stories hundreds of years later, as medieval scribes were writing from a patriarchal Christian perspective that frowned on female autonomy and free expressions of sexuality.

The position of the Celtic goddesses was also affected by the influx of beliefs that came with the Roman invasion of many Celtic regions. Deities were often Romanized to reflect the Empire's standards. Furthermore, the social position of women declined during the time of the invasion, as many Celts were forced to conform to Roman standards (McCoppin, 2022).

Consequently, Christian writers shifted and replaced symbols of divine women's regenerative sexuality with Christian images that portrayed them as chaste and submissive. Lubell (1994: 129) explains that:

> As deeply rooted ... Christian fear of the female came to prevail ... The patriarchy ... came to share an obsessive concern over women's "lust." This prurient concern gave birth not only to a suppression of imagery but to an intolerance of female sexuality.

As such, Christian writers altered the original stories of the goddesses to fit the social values of their society.

Below, we explore the stories of some of the most powerful female figures in Celtic mythology to consider why they were strong women and what their significance is today.

Rhiannon: Goddess of Sovereignty

What we know about the goddess Rhiannon comes from the Welsh *Mabinogion*. In that book of myths, she appears as one of the main female characters of the first "Pwyll" and the third "Manawydan" branch of the collection. Her persona is believed to have come from the pre-Christian goddesses Rigantona (meaning "great queen") and Epona, the horse goddess (MacKillop, 1998). According to Proinsias Mac Cana (1992), Rhiannon is the reincarnate of the goddess of sovereignty, who, by taking a spouse, ordained him as the legitimate king of the territory she personified.

This goddess is depicted in the *Mabinogion* as a strong-minded woman who comes from the Otherworld. One example of her independence in thought and action is her decision to choose Pwyll, Prince of Dyfed in West Wales as her husband instead of Gwawl, to whom she was originally betrothed. She is also depicted as intelligent, beautiful, politically strategic, and well-known for being wealthy and generous.

The story goes that Rhiannon, daughter of Hyfaidd Hen, was betrothed to Pwyll after he fell in love with her when he saw her ride by on a white horse. The Prince of Dyfed pursued her on horseback, but she outran him for three days. Afterward, she allowed him to catch up and agreed to marry him (Falkner, 2020). But after the wedding feast, he foolishly granted a wish to her rejected suitor, Gwawl, son of the goddess Clud (MacKillop, 1998). Naturally, Gwawl wished that Rhiannon would marry him. She told Pwyll to agree since he had no choice but to return at the end of the year on the occasion of her marriage feast and to bring a magical bag that she would give him.

When the feast came about, the prince attended with the object disguised as one of the servants. He then asked for his boon from Gwawl and that the bag be filled with food. However, it was enchanted, so it could never become full. When the groom asked why it wasn't filled yet, Pwyll replied that it would not be until a noble said: "Enough has been put in" (Ford,

1996: 212). When Gwawl stood up to do this, Pwyll trapped him in the bag. The prince's men, thinking it was a game of badger-in-the-bag, killed the trapped man.

This story demonstrates Rhiannon's determination to marry the man of her choice.

Rhiannon's character represents two archetypes of myth. The first of these is that of the gracious, bountiful queen goddess. The second is a wronged wife who is falsely accused of killing her son (Green, 2011). An example of the first occurs when the deity shows her true form as a goddess when she arrives at Pwyll's palace, Arberth, for the first time and dispenses precious gifts, revealing her divine origin (MacKillop, 1998).

The second archetype arose because of a situation that occurred a few years after Rhiannon and Pwyll's marriage. At that time, she had given birth to a son, who was stolen on May Eve, the night he was born and while he was under the care of his nursemaids. Fearing for their lives, the nursemaids, in desperation, killed a puppy and smeared the blood over Rhiannon's face (Falkner, 2020). She was then falsely accused of the infant's murder and obliged to do penance for seven years by sitting at the horse block outside the palace gate, offering all visitors a ride on her back.

But then, Teyrnon, Pwyll's retainer, realized that the child he had been fostering was a royal and returned him to his master and his wife. Rhiannon called the child Pryderi ("care") following her remark, "I should be delivered of my care if that were true," after Teyrnon told her that her child was alive and in his care (MacKillop, 1998).

This story shows how she did not lose her spirit despite being accused of one of the most heinous crimes. Pryderi also represents her role as the goddess of sovereignty, as he is the heir to his father's kingdom.

In the third branch of the *Mabinogion*, many years have passed, Pwyll has died, and Pryderi has inherited the kingdom. He then promises his mother as wife to his comrade in arms, Manawydan. Soon after, disaster begins to befall Dyfed and the royal family. A magical mist ravages the kingdom, leaving only Pryderi, his wife, Rhiannon, and Manawydan still living. Then, the mother and son are held hostage in Annwfn, and eventually freed by Manawydan.

Ultimately, the deadly mist is revealed to be the work of Llwyd, the enchanter, who was a friend of Gwawl's seeking revenge for the loss of Rhiannon to Pwyll. Following a comical set of magical negotiations about a pregnant mouse, Manawydan forces Llwyd to restore Dyfed to its former prosperity (MacKillop, 1998). This character's role in the story demonstrates how Rhiannon bestows sovereignty on her husbands.

Rhiannon's Association With Animals

Rhiannon is associated with horses and birds. Her links to the horse goddess Epona are demonstrated by the circumstances surrounding her meeting with Pwyll and the nature of her punishment when she is believed to have killed the infant Pryderi (MacKillop, 1998).

Falkner (2020) explains that Epona and Rhiannon are examples of regional variation in the Celtic religion. Horses played a key role in this world, both as a form of transport and in battle. In Ireland, Epona was the protector of horses, donkeys, and mules. Rhiannon may also be related to another Irish equine figure, Macha (MacKillop, 1998). Some sculptures of Epona show her with cornucopias and foals, suggesting that she was believed to influence fertility. The deity was popular among the calvary of the Roman Empire, especially with the Imperial Horse Guards, a royal group of elite riders. Rhiannon was her Welsh counterpart. Like her, Rhiannon protected horses but later evolved into the protector of the king and so became the goddess of sovereignty.

Blackbirds, of which the goddess is said to have three, are a symbol of Rhiannon's. They are partly of the Otherworld, as is she. Their association with this realm is demonstrated in the Welsh myth "Branwen, daughter of Llŷr," where the song of Rhiannon's blackbirds keeps Brân the Blessed and his companions in a state of timeless enchantment for 72 years (Byghan, 2020).

These three birds are also mentioned in the *Mabinogion* and are said to sing over the sea at Harlech. Also, in the story "Culhwch ac Olwen" ("How Culhwch Won Olwen"), they can wake the dead and lull the living to sleep (MacKillop, 1998). In the tale, the giant Ysbaddaden Bencawr demands that the hero Culhwch capture the birds to entertain him on the night before his death, an event that will immediately follow his daughter Olwen's marriage to Culhwch, after which the hero will inherit his late father-in-law's kingdom.

More generally in Celtic myth, the blackbird is described as a being with the power to send humans into dreamtime and able to speak with the dead (Carr-Gomm & Carr-Gomm, 1994).

The Morrígan: Goddess of War and Fate

The Morrígan ("the Great Queen" or "Phantom Queen") was a triple goddess associated with sovereignty, war, death, slaughter, and fate. She is the goddess of war and fury in early Irish tradition and embodied all that was perverse and horrible among the supernatural powers (Ellis, 1987). She was part of a trio of war goddesses called the Morrigna, along with Badb and Macha. Nemain is sometimes said to be part of the three, but she may be an aspect of Badb or The Morrígan.

Along with Badb and Macha, The Morrígan is a daughter of Ernmas. She may or may not be the wife or the consort of the Dagda, although it is certain that she had sexual relations with him. She is often described as living in the cave of Cruachain, County Roscommon, which is also the home of Medb (MacKillop, 1998).

As a war goddess, she does not engage in combat herself but rather has a psychological impact on armies, especially because of her frightful appearance. Her persona in many early Irish narratives, like "The Táin," combines her aggressive personality with an alluring sexuality. She also has the power of prophecy and can cast spells. Another belief is that she can predict who could win in battle and hovers over battlefields as a crow or raven (O'Hara, 2023; Sullivan, 2024).

The Morrígan is associated with wolves, ravens, and crows, the last of which she has a prominent connection with. She can turn herself into a bird, fish, or other animal, and she can transform from a beautiful young girl into a hag (MacKillop, 1998; Sullivan, 2024). She also took on the form of an eel when she had a magical battle with the hero, Cú Chulainn.

Her appearance in "The Táin," demonstrates many of the qualities she is associated with. In the tale, she first approaches Cú Chulainn as a femme fatale figure, appearing to him as a lovely young girl who wants him to make love to her. However, he rejects her, saying that he "does not have time for women's backsides" (MacKillop, 1998: 296). After first trying to seduce him, the goddess then fights with him, and he manages to wound her (Ellis, 1987). She then comes to him as an eel, a wolf, and a red hornless heifer but fails to seduce him in any of her forms. Instead, he breaks the ribs of the eel, pulls an eye out of the wolf, and breaks the leg of the heifer (MacKillop, 1998).

Later, when The Morrígan sees the hero in combat, she approaches him as an old milch cow. When he asks her for a drink, she allows him to suckle from each of her three teats. She then tells Cú Chulainn that he will die when the calf of the cow is a yearling. To help matters along, she breaks the wheels of his chariot. In the end, she appears on his shoulder as a hooded crow, signifying the scavenging of his corpse while a beaver drinks his blood (MacKillop, 1998; Ellis, 1987).

The Morrígan is also said to have helped Dé Danann at the battle of Magh Tuireadh and appeared to Conaire Mór before his death at Dá Derga's hostel (Ellis, 1987).

Womanly Power and Wisdom

The Morrígan's appearance to Cú Chulainn in "The Táin" is of particular interest and helps us understand and appreciate the power and influence goddesses and, by extension, women, had in Celtic society. As the deity of death and fertility, her appearance to the hero of the tale serves to teach him the futility of fighting against what she represents. Up until the point that he met her, he was able to defy all odds and overcome all adversities single-handedly.

She taught him about the cycle of life, as her various appearances to him represented the life stage he embodied at each time. For example, when the hero was young and strong, he saw her as a maiden. When he felt the fury of battle, he saw her in fearsome animal forms, and when he felt "great weariness" after ceaseless fighting, he saw the goddess as an old woman (McCoppin, 2022). These symbolic lessons about the life cycle allow Cú Chulainn to accept the inevitability of his death.

However, as a fertility goddess, The Morrígan also teaches the hero that nature's cycle leads to the renewal of all living beings. She showed him this when his drinking of her milk healed the wounds that he had inflicted on her (McCoppin, 2022).

Thus, it can be argued that the goddess holds central authority within "The Táin" because her impact on the hero is not matched by any male character within the text. In this context, The Morrígan is portrayed in a powerful light, as she imparts vital wisdom to the male hero. This is a common theme in Celtic mythology, demonstrating the high regard the Celts often had for their goddesses (McCoppin, 2022).

Ceridwen: Goddess of Poetry, Magic, and Transformation

Ceridwen, also spelled Cerridwen, Caridwen, Keridwen, or Kryrridwen meaning "white" or "blessed," was a shape-shifting keeper of a cauldron of wisdom called Awen at the bottom of the Bala Lake (or Llyn Tegid) in north Wales (MacKillop, 1998). For this reason, she is remembered as the goddess of magic.

Her cauldron was symbolic of her power, and similar items are commonplace in Celtic legend. The vessel is also a symbol of the Otherworld. The knowledge and powers of Ceridwen are similar to those of the Salmon of Knowledge in Irish legend, as explored in the story of Fionn mac Cumhaill (Wright, 2022).

She was a Welsh sorceress and is portrayed as one of the most powerful witches in Celtic mythology. Ceridwen is both a mother and a wise woman gifted with poetic wisdom, prophecy, and inspiration, with these three latter qualities known collectively as *awen* in Welsh lore. Her powers came from her magic cauldron, in which she brewed potions to help others, although she possessed many of these abilities herself without needing its power. She was also in possession of a magical throne, which was the source of her sovereignty and some of her strength (Wright, 2022).

Ceridwen's husband was Tegid Foel ("the bald") and among her children were a beautiful daughter, Creirwy, and the ugly Morfran, her son (also called Afagddu). She is often depicted as a witch or an unpleasant hag, but she is also sometimes depicted as a goddess, specifically as a sovereignty goddess or a creator (MacKillop, 1998; Wright, 2022).

She is said to have produced a range of potions in Awen. Some changed the appearance of other people, perhaps giving the person who drank it the ability to shapeshift; others gave the drinker the gift of awen itself. While many of her potions granted great gifts to those who drank them, they could also be dangerous. For example, after the gift is given, a single drop has the power to kill. This made her careful about whom she gave her potions to, as she did not want to harm others and knew that her powers came with a price (Wright, 2022).

The goddess is a white witch, meaning that she used her gifts and her cauldron to help others. Her motivations are mostly altruistic, but she also uses her power to help her friends and family. This motivation mostly manifests in her attempts to help Morfran. Sometimes, her ploys backfire or don't work out, and she lets anger overtake her; however, she manages to calm down before she does anything she will later regret (Wright, 2022).

Ceridwen, Poetry, and Myth

The association between Ceridwen and poetry may have its roots in a tradition begun by Taliesin, an early Brittonic poet of sub-Roman Britain who lived around the sixth century C.E. His works survive in the Middle Welsh manuscript the *Book of Taliesin.* He saw the goddess as a giver of inspiration, and his poems are full of references to Ceridwen, such as:

- I obtained my inspiration/ From the Cauldron of Ceridwen ("History of Taliesin" cited by Matthews, 2002: 78), and

- Conspicuous when came from the Cauldron/ The Three Inspirations of Ogyrwen.../Mine is the splendid Chair,/ The inspiration of my ardent song ("The Royal Chair" cited by Matthews, 2002: 78).

These poems hint at how she was the goddess of inspiration. Some have suggested that the reference to "Ogyrwen" in "The Royal Chair" refers to a god of poetry or inspiration; however, Matthews (2002) disagrees with this, instead proposing that the word is a title that was applied specifically to Cerdiwen as the goddess of inspiration.

One interesting story links the mythical Ceridwen to the real-life poet Taliesin. It is said that three magical drops from a potion that was intended for Morfran fell instead on Gwion Bach, who had been tasked with stirring the liquid as it was brewing in the cauldron. This gave him unique wisdom and insight and led to Ceridwen pursuing him. Both pursuer and pursued frequently changed shape during the chase: Gwion Bach changed into a hare, Cerdiwen into a greyhound, and so forth. Eventually, he turned into a grain of wheat and Ceridwen swallowed him, becoming pregnant as a result. Nine months later, the child born to her was Taliesin (MacKillop, 1998).

This story hints at the strong link between goddess and poet. It also evokes a sense of him gaining inspiration from her as a maternal figure, as mothers give life to their children. Also, Ceridwen engages in shape shifting throughout this story, demonstrating her role as the goddess of transformation.

Deirdre of the Sorrows: Love Over Duty

Deirdre (also known as Derdriu, Deirdriu, Deidri, and Derdreend) is the tragic heroine of the *Ulster Cycle* whose best-known narrative is one of the "Three Sorrows of Storytelling" of the Irish tradition. The Irish text of her story, "*Longas mac nUislenn*" ("The Exile of the Sons of Uisnech") survives in several works, including the 12th-century *Book of Leinster* and the *Yellow Book of Lecan* as well as in a prologue to "The Táin" (MacKillop, 1998). In the *Ulster Cycle*, Deirdre is not just tragic and beautiful—she is also a catalyst for vengeance and misfortune for the nobility and warriors of the province.

Deirdre was the daughter of Felim Mac Dall, a chieftain of Ulster, and was born when he was entertaining the King of Ulster, Conchobar Mac Nessa, at his fortress. Cathbad the Druid cast the newborn Deirdre's horoscope and said that she would be the fairest of all the women in Ireland and would wed a king. However, he also foretold that, because of her, only death and ruin would come upon the land.

Conchobar's warriors wanted the baby to be put to death at once, but the king saved the child, excited by the prospect of her future beauty, saying that he would raise her, and when she was old enough, she would be his wife. According to Conchobar, if she was married to him, no foreign monarch could wed her, so she could not cause any war or division in Ulster (Ellis, 1987).

But when Deirdre came of age, she realized that she did not want to marry an old man. She also fell in love with a man her age. One day, looking over the ramparts of Emain Macha, she saw a handsome young warrior. The young lady asked her nurse (some stories say foster father and that he was a forester), Leabharcham, to identify him. She learned that the man was Naoise, son of Usna, a hero of the Red Branch. Deirdre engineered a meeting, and the two fell in love. They then eloped with the help of Naoise's brothers, Ainle and Ardan, and fled to Alba (Ellis, 1987; MacKillop, 1998).

There, the sons of Usna went into the service of the king of Cruithne. For a while, the couple lived happily together in Glen Etive. Some versions of the story say that, at this time, they had two children, a son Gaiar, and a daughter, Aebgriene (Monaghan, 2004). The children were fostered by Manannán mac Lir (Hitt, 1908).

As the years went by, Conchobar became increasingly bitter. Outwardly though, he pretended to forgive Deirdre and Naoise. He sent Fergus mac Róich to invite them to return to Ulster in peace. Deirdre, having foreseen doom, did not want to; however, Naoise trusted Fergus, as he knew him to be a man of his word, so they returned to Ulster. Once Conchobar had confirmed that Deirdre was as beautiful as ever, he sent his warriors to attack the hostel of the Red Branch where she and her party were staying. The attackers then murdered Naoise and killed or bribed everyone else, and she was forced to wed Conchobar (Ellis, 1987).

For a year, Deirdre was his unwilling wife, never smiling. Conchobar, angered by her attitude, asked her who she hated most in the world. "You and Éogan mac Durthacht!" she replied, referencing the man who had killed her first husband (Ellis, 1987: 81).

Enraged, Conchobar told her she would be Éogan's wife for a year. But when she was placed in the man's chariot with her hands tied behind her back to prevent her from escaping, she contrived to fling herself headfirst from it, hitting her skull on a rock and killing herself. In other versions of the story, she fatally stabs herself with a knife, throwing it into the sea so that no one else will be blamed for her death (MacKillop, 1998).

Deirdre's fate was tragic, but the spirit she displayed in defying her captors is admirable.

Conchobar's behavior toward her and Naoise meant that his followers began to view him as untrustworthy. As a result, many of his best warriors deserted him for Ailill and Medb of Connacht and fought against him in "The Táin," bringing about Cathbad's prophecy (MacKillop, 1998).

Oral tradition says that Deirdre and Naoise are buried together at Armagh. Conchobar is said to have driven two yew stakes between the graves, but these later grew together and intertwined with each other as a symbol of the couple's eternal love for one another (MacKillop, 1998).

Legend of Love and Lust—Deirdre's Legacy in Portrayals of Female Sexuality

In the early 20th century, as part of the Celtic revival, Deirdre's story was reworked by several playwrights including George William Russell, W.B. Yeats, and J.M. Synge. Russell's and Yeats's plays, *Deirdre* (1902) and *Deirdre* (1907) respectively, contain sensuality as a central theme and harken back to an idealized peasant life before industrialization (Redwine, 2021).

However, J.M. Synge's play, *Deirdre of the Sorrows* (1910) underlies the subject matter with a far more physical, crude sexuality. The three-act play was based on Irish mythology, particularly the legend of Deirdre and her marriages to Naoise and Conchobar. The play was unfinished when Synge died on March 24, 1909, so it was completed by W.B. Yeats with the assistance of Synge's fiancée, Molly Allgood, the following year (Synge, 1935).

In the text, Synge mixes melancholy with a raw, sensual element to humanize the subject matter. To this end, Synge's Deirdre embodies physical sexuality. In the play, Lavarcham—the text's counterpart of Deirdre's nurse, Leabharcham—describes her charge as nakedly physical "Bathing in the sun ... with her white skin and her red lips and the blue water and the ferns about her" (Redwine, 2021: 102). The character also speaks of Naisi (Naoise) in striking, physical language: "Naisi is it? I didn't care if the crows were stripping his thigh-bones at the dawn of day" (Redwine, 2021: 102).

Thus, Synge portrays the lovers with raw sensuality, adding a sexual depth to their tragic love story.

Here, Synge associates Deirdre's sexuality with power, as she is portrayed as single-minded in her rejection of the much older Conchobar in favor of the young, attractive Naisi, even though she knows that it will mean death for both her and her lover (Finney, 1989).

Summary

This exploration of powerful female figures in Celtic mythology has shown that, despite the efforts of the Romans and medieval scribes to diminish the role women played in Celtic society, these goddesses remained powerful figures in legend. Rhiannon demonstrated power with her ability to grant sovereignty to her husbands. Meanwhile, The Morrígan used her links to death and fertility to share her wisdom with Cú Chulainn and instruct him about and help him accept the things he could not defeat. Ceridwen was a powerful sorceress who used her powers for good and gave others the power of inspiration, while Deirdre experienced many sorrows but remained determined to marry and remain true to the man that she loved rather than be forced into a marriage with the elderly King Conchobar.

With that, we are almost at the end of our study of powerful women in Celtic history. The next chapter will explore what we have learned about Celtic women, their power in the world, and what lessons and inspiration we can take from their stories today.

Chapter Seven
Conclusion

A Celtic woman is often the equal of any Roman man in hand-to-hand combat. She is as beautiful as she is strong. Her body is comely but fierce. The physiques of our Roman women pale in comparison. – Unidentified Roman Soldier

IN THIS BOOK, WE learned about courageous Celtic female leaders, both historical and mythological. They came from a culture that viewed women as being equal in value to men. As such, Celtic women played prominent roles in their society, with many undertaking what are generally perceived to be male roles. Some were warriors, and others functioned in leadership roles specifically designated for women, such as seeresses like Veleda.

The loss of Celtic matrilineal traditions had an enduring impact on women's equality due to the transition to a patriarchal society after the Roman Conquest, as the invaders did not believe that women were capable of filling leadership positions. Then, after Europe's conversion to Christianity, pagan traditions were absorbed into Christian cultures, and their emphasis on women's empowerment was lost until it found new appreciation in the 20th century.

Today, the legacy of Celtic female empowerment is more relevant than ever. Although we see history as progressive, there is a possibility that we are in actuality relearning the wisdom of a more enlightened era of ancient history. Examples from the Celtic period have taught us that any woman can perform roles traditionally held by men and do them just as well and, in some cases, better. As Ammianus Marcellinus later recalled, Celtic female warriors were generally considered far more intimidating and were feared by the Romans far more than their husbands.

Below, we discuss what the lives and legacies of these women have taught us and what can be gleaned from the memorable and inspirational accounts of these individuals.

What These Women Can Teach Us

In each of the five chapters of this book, we learned something from accounts of these women and so their stories can teach us something.

In the first chapter, we looked at the lives of Boudica, Queen of the Iceni, and Medb, the mythological Queen of Connacht. Each ruled in her own right. Boudica led armies into battle after the Romans had tried to take over her lands and had violated her daughters, while Medb was a powerful, autonomous queen who did as she pleased. Both these women suffered defeat in battle: Boudica against the overwhelming power and organization of the Romans and Medb in "The Táin." Despite this, they were in a position of real power and remain shining examples of female leadership, autonomy, and strength.

In the second chapter, we briefly explored the stories of Scáthach, the warrior queen, and her sister and rival, Aífe. The stories told about both these women show that independent women could live and thrive without men in the Celtic period. Some modern historians have accused them of being "indifferent" to men; however, such comments seem overly harsh (Ross, 1970). Instead, their independence should be celebrated.

We also learned that not all warrior women relied on combat alone. Instead, historical examples such as Cartimandua, Queen of the Brigantes, should be remembered for their skills in peacemaking and diplomacy. Today, this ruler is unfairly judged for her loyalty to the Romans. However, her allegiance could also be viewed as being in the best interests of her subjects, as her domains enjoyed a period of prosperity under her rule that lasted until she was ousted by her ex-husband and co-ruler after she left him for another man. Another example from myth, Liath Luachra, was also a Druidess warrior but is mainly remembered for her role in bringing up and protecting the hero Fionn mac Cumhaill.

These examples also show how Celtic female leaders had a semi-divine status. Examples include Boudica worship and attendance of the cult of Andraste, and Scáthach and Aífe's involvement through sex in the sacred initiation of Cú Chulainn as a warrior. Another example is Brigid, who was originally a goddess and, later, due to her influence, reimagined as a Christian saint.

Other examples that have been explored highlight the power and influence of female seers and prophetesses in Celtic society, as proven by the historical examples of Veleda and Ganna. The former in particular is remembered for her role in negotiations between her tribe and the Romans. The significant role of prophetesses in Celtic society is mirrored in myth in the examples of Macha and Fedelm.

How Their Stories Inspire Us

One thing that is apparent from these examples is that a woman does not have to be a warrior or fulfill a political role in society to be powerful. Many of the examples of powerful women explored here are remembered for their roles as wise women, such as Veleda, Ganna, and Ceridwen, or as nurturing, maternal figures, such as Brigid or Liath Luachra. Celtic women were also considered to be powerful if they had the power to inspire others, such as poets. Two notable examples are again Brigid and Ceridwen. They teach us that you can be powerful as a creative or as a nurturer as much as if your strengths lie in the areas of fighting and diplomacy.

Celtic women, both real and mythological are seen as symbols of empowerment because they inspired respect (and fear). Women such as Boudica, Cartimandua, Medb, and Veleda were capable of dealing with conflict and resistance, were resilient, and were also bestowers of wisdom and prophecy.

Today's leaders can learn a lot from ancient Celtic women, such as the need to govern with courage, wisdom, and compassion, not just protecting the interests of the privileged but representing all members of society. Celtic female leaders still inspire modern women seeking reconnection with lost ancient matriarchal values, rites, rituals, and practices, which allowed women to occupy more empowered roles. Through learning about Celtic female leaders, we can reclaim women's place in history by exploring and appreciating the legacy of these powerful Celtic examples.

Unfortunately, the stories of such women are mostly lost to us today. If you agree that this is an oversight that needs to be addressed, continue to search and read about their forgotten stories and hidden histories. We should be proud of the historical achievement of women's leadership and forces for change and equality throughout history.

If you have enjoyed reading this book, please take a moment to give it a quick review and rating on Amazon. This is so helpful in boosting its visibility. To make this quick and easy for you, just scan the QR code of your country's marketplace to take you straight to the 'leave a review' section. Many thanks again for choosing to read this book, and please keep your eye out for upcoming books in this series.

Elise

Have a look at the other books in the Brave Women in History series by visiting my website: www.ReadEliseBaker.com
and do sign up for my monthly newsletter to receive a your free eBook as a gift. Thank you!

US: Leave a review on amazon.com:

UK: Leave a review on amazon.co.uk:

Australia: Leave a review on amazon.com.au:

Canada: To leave a review on amazon.ca:

About the Author

Elise Baker

Elise Baker has a lifelong interest in women's history and feminism. She holds an Honors degree and a Postgraduate Diploma that led to a career as a librarian, archivist, and eventually an editor for television. She loves traveling to different countries and experiencing diverse cultures. When she's not reading or writing, she enjoys walking with her dog along the beach and seeing plays at the theater with family and friends.

Elise's maternal family, from the borderlands of the Czech Republic, became refugees with no country to belong to after the Second World War and dispersed all over the world. She grew up listening to her grandmother's recollections of this time and believes that understanding and learning from the bravery of ordinary women is essential in shaping the future.

Her passion is excavating the past to unearth the stories of women whose remarkable feats and accomplishments have been buried and forgotten because of their gender. Her sincere hope is that they can fuel and inspire women of today to face adversity and discrimination with courage. She enjoys bringing to light stories that celebrate history beyond the usual narratives.

In learning about the achievements of these remarkable women, we address the serious shortage of women in documented history. There are countless women leaders whose contributions have been forgotten. Often, they put their lives on the line, knowing that their efforts would likely go unrecognized. Their stories offer a more balanced perspective on history. May they serve as inspiration to women to continue to make a difference and occupy important spaces.

To see more books in the Brave Women in History and the Brave Women Who Changed the Course of WWII series,
please visit: www.ReadEliseBaker.com or scan the QR code below.

Also By

To keep an eye out for new titles, bringing more forgotten stories of women's achievements to light,
and to sign up for Elise Baker's monthly newsletter **Brave Women in History** please visit: https://www.ReadEliseBaker.com
or scan the QR code below.

Blazing the Way: Match Girls, Mill Girls and Other Fiery Females Whose Strikes Sparked a Revolution in Women's Rights

Voices of Freedom: Harriet Tubman, Sojourner Truth, and Other Women Abolitionists Who Shattered Chains

Princess, Countess, Socialite, Spy: True Stories of High-Society Ladies Turned WWII Spies

Women Code Breakers: The Best Kept Secret of WWII True Stories of Female Code Breakers Whose Top-Secret Work Helped Win World War II

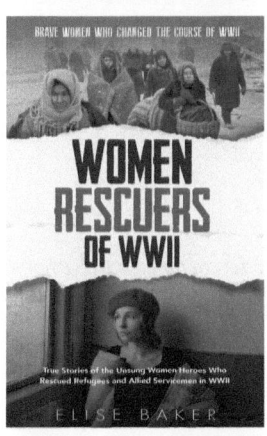

Women Rescuers of WWII: True Stories of the Unsung Women Heroes Who Rescued Refugees and Allied Servicemen in WWII

Nightingales, Bluebirds and Angels of Mercy: True Stories of the Courage and Heroism of Nurses on the Front Line in WWII

References and Bibliography

Anderson, E. N. (2014). *Caring for place: Ecology, ideology, and emotion in traditional landscape management.* Routledge.

Barnett, D. (2023). *Boudicca returns as a 21st-century feminist—2,000 years after her death.*
The Guardian.
https://www.theguardian.com/uk-news/2023/apr/02/boudicca-returns-as-a-21st-century-feminist-2000-years-after-her-death

Berg, S. (2022). *Brigid: The Celtic goddess who became a saint.* Creek Ridge Publishing.

Bernhardt-House, P. A. (2009). Warriors, words, and wood: Oral and literary wisdom in the exploits of Irish mythological warriors. *Studia Celtica Fennica, 6:* 5-19.

Bero, T. (2023). *How St. Brigid became a powerful feminist symbol in Ireland.* CBC News.
https://www.cbc.ca/radio/tapestry/how-st-brigit-became-a-powerful-feminist-symbol-in-ireland-1.6777531

Birley, A. (1980). *The people of Roman Britain.* University of California Press.

Blackie, S. (2019). *If women rose rooted: A life-changing journey to authenticity and belonging.* September Publishing.

Byghan, Y. (2020). *Sacred and mythological animals: A worldwide taxonomy.* McFarland & Company.

Carlyle, T. (1841). *On heroes, hero-worship, & the heroic in history: Six lectures.* James Fraser.

Carr-Gomm, P., & Carr-Gomm, S. (1994). *The Druid animal oracle: Working with the sacred animals of the Druid tradition.* Fireside.

Cartwright, M. (2021). Sacred sites & rituals in the ancient Celtic religion. *World History Encyclopedia.* https://www.worldhistory.org/article/1710/sacred-sites--rituals-in-the-ancient-celtic-religi/

Condren, M. (1989). *The serpent and the goddess: Women, religion, and power in Celtic Ireland.* Harper & Row.

Cross, R., & Miles, R., (2011). *Warrior women: Years of courage and heroism.* Metro Books.

Cunliffe, B. W. (1978). *Iron Age communities in Britain: An account of England, Scotland, and Wales from the seventh century BC until the Roman conquest.* Routledge & Kegan Paul.

Curran, B. (2010). *Mysteries of Celtic mythology in American folklore.* Pelican Publishing.

Davies, J. A. (2008). *The land of Boudica: Prehistoric and Roman Norfolk.* Oxford Books.

Delamarre, X. (2003). *Dictionnaire de la langue gauloise: Une approche linguistique du vieux-celtique continental.* Errance.

Depuis, N. (2009). *Mna na hEireann: Women who shaped Ireland.* Mercier Press.

The Editors of Encyclopedia Britannica. (2024a). The cattle raid of Cooley. Britannica.
https://www.britannica.com/topic/The-Cattle-Raid-of-Cooley

The Editors of Encyclopedia Britannica. (2024b).
Brigit: Celtic deity. Britannica.
https://www.britannica.com/topic/Brigit

Elliott, S. (2021). *Britain: Roman conquests.* Pen & Sword.
Ellis, P. B. (1987). *A dictionary of Irish mythology.* Constable.
Enright, M. J. (1996). *Lady with a mead cup.* Four Courts Press.
Estes, C. P. (2008). *Women who run with the wolves: Contracting the power of the wild woman.* Rider.
Eyres, K. (2007). *Celtic myth.* Flame Tree Publishing.
Falkner, D. E. (2020). *The mythology of the night sky: Greek, Roman, and other celestial law* (2nd ed.). Springer.
Finney, G. (1989). *Women in modern drama: Freud, feminism, and European theater at the turn of the century.* Cornell University Press.
Flisiuk, F. (2015). The role and power of women in Irish culture: As illustrated in "The Tain." *Every Corner: A Story.* https://franman3024.tumblr.com/post/82118941671/the-role-and-power-of-women-in-irish-culture
Ford, P. K. (1996). Prolegomena to a reading of the *Mabinogi*: "Pwyll" and "Manawydan." In C. W. Sullivan (Ed.), *The Mabinogi: A book of essays.* Garland Publishing, Inc.
Fowler, W. W. (2020). *Religious experience of the Roman people.* Outlook.
Frankel, V. E. (2015). *The symbolism and sources of* Outlander*: The Scottish fairies, folklore, ballads, magic, and meanings that inspired the series.* McFarland & Company.
Fraser, A. (1988). *The warrior queens: Boudicea's chariot.* Viking.
Frazer, J. G. (1947). *The golden bough: A study in magic and religion.* The Macmillan Company.
French, C. (2020). *Ancient Gaelic women-Priestesses, wise women, herbal experts, warriors, royal rulers.* Hub Pages. https://discover.hubpages.com/politics/Ancient-Gaelic-Women-Priestesses-Wise-Women-Herbal-Experts-Warriors-Royal-Rulers
Frenee-Hutchins, S. (2014). *Boudica's odyssey in early modern England.* Routledge.
Grant, M. (1974). *The army of the Caesars.* Charles Scribner's Sons.
Grant, M. (1995). *Greek and Roman historians: Information and misinformation.* Routledge.

Green, M. J. (1997). *Exploring the world of the Druids.* Thames & Hudson.

Green, M. (2011). *The gods of the Celts.* History Press.

Guiley, R. (2008). *The encyclopedia of witches, witchcraft, and Wicca* (3rd ed.). Facts On File.

Heinz, S. (1997). *Celtic symbols.* Sterling Publishing Company, Inc.

Heinz, S. (2010). Afterlife and Celtic concepts of the otherworld. In L. Sikorska (Ed.), *Thise stories beren witnesse: The landscape of the afterlife in medieval and post-medieval imagination.* Peter Lang.

Henderson, J. G. W. (1998). *A Roman life: Rutilius Gallicus on paper and in stone.* University of Exeter Press.

Henshall, K. (2008). *Folly and fortune in early British history: From Caesar to the Normans.* Palgrave Macmillan.

Hingley, R. (2022). *Conquering the ocean: The Roman invasion of Britain.* Oxford University Press.

Hingley, R., & Unwin, C. (2005). *Boudica: Iron Age warrior queen.* Hambledon Continuum.

History Brought Alive. (2022). *Celtic mythology & history: Explore timeless tales, folklore, magic, legendary stories, & more.* History Brought Alive.

Hitt, J. G. (1908). *Deirdre and the Sons of Uisneach: A Scoto-Irish romance of the first century A.D.* Marshall Brothers.

Hoffman, B. (2019). *The Roman invasion of Britain: Archaeology versus history.* Pen & Sword.

Howarth, N. (2008). *Cartimandua: Queen of the Brigandes.* History Press.

Irby-Massie, G. L. (1999). *Military religion in Roman Britain.* Brill.

Irslinger, B. (2013). Medb "the intoxicating one"? (Re-)constructing the past through etymology. *Ulidia 4: Proceedings of the Fourth International Conference on the Ulster Cycle of Tales.*

Jackson, G. M. (1990). *Women who ruled.* Clio Press.

Kelly, P. (1992). The Tain as literature. In J. P. Mallory (Ed.), *Aspects of the Tain.* Belfast.

Klimczak, N. (2016). *Female Druids, the forgotten priestesses of the Celts.* Ancient Origins. https://www.ancient-origins.net/history/female-druids-forgotten-priestesses-celts-005910

Koch, J. T. (Ed.). (2006). *Celtic culture: A historical encyclopedia*. ABC-CLIO.

Koch, J. T. & Carey, J. (Eds.). (2000). *The Celtic heroic age*. Andover.

LAMDA. (2019). *Boudica*. London Academy of Music & Dramatic Art. https://www.lamda.ac.uk/whats-on/boudica

Lehmann, E. (2008). "And thus I will it": Queen Medb and the will to power. *Proceedings of the Harvard Celtic Colloquium* 28: 142-151.

Lendering, J. (2006). *Veleda*. Livius. https://www.livius.org/articles/person/veleda/

Lewis, J. J. (2017). *Cartimandua, Brigandtine queen and peacemaker*. ThoughtCo. https://www.thoughtco.com/cartimandua-brigantine-queen-biography-3530255

Lubell, W. M. (1994). *The metamorphosis of Baubo: Myths of women's sexual energy*. Vanderbilt University Press.

Lysaght, P. (1986). *The banshee: The Irish supernatural death-messenger*. Glendale Press.

Mac Cana, P. (1992). *The Mabinogi*. University of Wales Press.

MacCullouch, J. A., Rolleston, T. W., & Evans-Wentz, W. Y. (2023). *Celtic mythology*. DigiCat.

MacKillop, J. (1998). *Dictionary of Celtic mythology*. Oxford University Press.

MacLeod, S. P. (2014). *The divine feminine in ancient Europe: Goddesses, sacred women, and the origins of Western culture*. McFarland & Company.

Mallory, J. P. & Adams, D. Q. (Eds.). (1997). *Encyclopedia of Indo-European culture*. Fitzroy Dearborn Publishers.

Markale, J. (1984). *The epics of Celtic Ireland: Ancient tales of mystery and magic*. Inner Traditions International, Ltd.

Markale, J. (1986). *Women of the Celts*. Inner Traditions International, Ltd.

Matson, G. (2004). *Celtic mythologies A to Z*. Facts on File.

Matthews, J. (2002). *Taliesin: The last Celtic shaman*. Inner Traditions.

McCoppin, R. S. (2022). *Goddess lost: How the downfall of female deities downgraded women's status in world cultures.* McFarland & Company.

Meyer, K. (1888). The wooing of Emer. *Archaeological Review,* 1: 68-75; 150-155; 231-235; 298-307.

Meyer, K. (1897). The cherishing of Conall Cernach and the deaths of Ailill and Conall Cernach. *Zeitschrift für celtische Philologie,* 1: 102–111

Meyer, K. (1904). The death of Conla. *Eriu,* 1: 113-121.

Monaghan, P. (2004). *The encyclopedia of Celtic mythology and folklore.* Facts on File, Inc.

Morris, K. (1991). *Sorceress or witch? The image of gender in medieval Iceland and Northern Europe.* University Press of America.

Neill, J. (2009). *The origins and role of same-sex relations in human societies.* McFarland & Company.

NicGrioghair, B. (2024). Bridget, bright goddess of the Gael. *Mythical Ireland.* https://mythicalireland.com/blogs/myths-legends/bridget-bright-goddess-of-the-gael

O'Donohue, J. (1999) *Anam Cara: Spiritual Wisdom from the Celtic World.* Bantam.

O'Donohue, J. (2000) *Eternal Echoes: Exploring Our Hunger to Belong.* Bantam.

O'Hara, K. (2023). *11 major Celtic gods and goddesses.* The Irish Road Trip. https://www.theirishroadtrip.com/celtic-gods-and-goddesses/

O'Neill, J. (1905). Cath Boinde. *Eriu,* 2: 173-185.

O'Rahilly, C. (1975). *Tain bo cualgne recension 1.* Corpus of Electronic Texts. https://celt.ucc.ie/published/T301012/index.html

Parker, G. (2016). Foreigners and Flavians: Prejudices and engagements. In A. Zissos (Ed.), *A companion to the Flavian age of imperial Rome.* John Wiley & Sons.

Peck, H. T. (1965). *Harper's dictionary of classical literature and antiquities* (2nd ed.). Cooper Square Publishers, Inc.

Penczak, C. (2007). *The temple of high witchcraft: Ceremonies, spheres, and the witches' qabalah.* Llewellyn Publications.

Pennington, R. (2003). *Amazons and fighter pilots: A biographical dictionary of military women*. Greenwood Press.

Pinault, G. J. (2007). Gaulois Epomeduos, le maitre des chevaux. In P.Y. Lambert and G.J. Pinault (Eds.), *Gaulois et celtique continental*. Droz.

Potter, T. W. (2004). Boudicca (d. AD 60/61). *Oxford Dictionary of National Biography*.
https://doi.org/10.1093/ref:odnb/2732

Pratt, C. (2007). *An encyclopedia of shamanism*. The Rosen Publishing Group, Inc.

Puhvel, J. (1970). *Myth and law among the Indo-Europeans: Studies in Indo-European comparative mythology*. University of California Press.

Redwine, E. B. (2021). *Gender, performance, and authorship at the Abbey Theatre*. Oxford University Press.

Roberts, A. (2024). *Cartimandua, queen of the Brigantes*. English Heritage.
https://www.english-heritage.org.uk/learn/histories/women-in-history/cartimandua/

Rogers, K., & Niemchick, A. (2023). Celtic region: Beliefs, practices, and institutions.
Britannica. https://www.britannica.com/topic/human-body-systems-2237111

Rolleston, T. W. (1986). *Celtic myths and legends*. Gresham.

Rose, S. O. (2010). *What is gender history?* Polity Press.

Ross, A. (1970). *Everyday life of the pagan Celts*. Carousel Books.

Rua, A. (2008). *Celtic flame: An insider's guide to Irish pagan tradition*. iUniverse.

Scholarly Community Encyclopedia. (2024). *List of women warriors in folklore*. https://encyclopedia.pub/entry/32556

Shephard, R. J. (2015). *An illustrated history of health and fitness, from pre-history to our post-modern world*. Springer.

Simek, R. (2020). Encounters: Roman. In J. P. Schjodt, J. Lindow, & A. Andren (Eds.), *The pre-Christian religions of the north, history, and structures: Vol. II*. Brepols.

Simmons, V. (2012). Tattooing. In J.T. Koch, & A. Minard (Eds.), *The Celts: History, life, and culture, Vol. 1*. ABC-CLIO.

Smith, A. (1996). Introduction. In A. Smith (Ed.), *Collected Plays, poems, and the Aran Islands*. Everyman.

Snyder, C. A. (2003). *The Britons*. Blackwell.

Sullivan, N. (2024). *A beginner's guide to Celtic spirituality: An introduction to Celtic spiritual mysteries, myths, and rituals*. Self-published.

Symonds, M. (2017). *Cartimandua's capital: Roman diplomacy and the rise of Stanwick*. Current Archaeology. https://archaeology.co.uk/articles/features/cartimanduas-capital.htm

Synge, J. M. (1935). *The complete plays*. Vintage Books.

Tanishka. (2017). *Goddess wisdom: Connect to the power of the sacred feminine through ancient teachings and practices*. Hay House Publishers.

Telyndru, J. (2023). *The ninefold way of Avalon: Walking the path of the priestess*. Llewellyn Publications.

Tristram, H. L. C. (1998). *Neue methoden der epenforschung*. Gunter Narr Verlag.

Van der Hoeven, J. (2017). *Pagan portals: The crane bag: A Druid's guide to ritual tools and practices*. John Hunt Publishing.

Vandrei, M. (2018). *Queen Boudica and historical culture in Britain: An image of truth*. Oxford University Press.

Visit Armagh. (2024). *The curse of Macha*. https://visitarmagh.com/stories/live-our-celtic-myths-legends-in-the-ancient-site-of-navan-fort/the-curse-of-macha/

Wall, M. (2022). *The lost battlefields of Britain*. Amberley.

Walsh, A. (2015). *Ancient Celtic women*. Medium. https://medium.com/legendary-women/ancient-celtic-women-7ee12e3dca01

Watts, D. (2005). *Boudicca's heirs: Women in early Britain*. Routledge.

Weber, C. (2015). *Brigid: History, mystery, and magick of the Celtic goddess*. Weiser Books.

Webster, G. (1978). *Boudica, the British revolt against Rome AD 60*. Rowman & Littlefield.

Webster, G. (1993). *The Roman invasion of Britain, revised edition*. Routledge.

Wilker, J. (2023). Sociae et amicae populi Romani: Women and the institution of client kingship. In H. Cornwell, & G. Woolf (Eds.), *Gendering Roman imperialism*. Brill.

Williamson, J. & McMenemy, G. (2023). *Women of myth*. Adams Media.

Wright, G. (2022). Ceridwen. *Mythopedia*. https://mythopedia.com/topics/ceridwen

Wyatt, D. R. (2009). *Slaves and warriors in medieval Britain and Ireland: 800-1200*. Brill.

www.ingramcontent.com/pod-product-compliance
Lightning Source LLC
Chambersburg PA
CBHW060616080526
44585CB00013B/850